Decode Your Brilliance™

A Guide to Unleashing Your Unique Advantage

By Vanessa Siliezar

ISBN: 979-8-9858450-8-2

Publisher: Mariposa Sources, Moreno Valley, CA

Proprietary Rights Clause:

To My Niece:

This is dedicated to you, for your first birthday.

You brought joy back into the family.

May your dreams come true, just believe in yourself

.

Acknowledgements

No one builds a business - or writes a book - alone.

To the MBA students who appointed me, an undergrad, as team lead during our consultancy project in England: you sparked a fire in me that has never gone out.

To Michael MacQueen at the University of Redlands, who took a fledgling idea and transformed it into the School of Business consulting capstone, giving me the opportunity to tackle an international consultancy project during my bachelor program and a domestic consultancy project during my master's program, thank you for believing in the power of practical learning.

To Jim Spee at the University of Redlands, who once told me that my brilliance wouldn't be fully recognized until I left the University as an employee. You were right - and I'm grateful for the push.

To Jim Pick, who introduced me to the world of publishing by trusting me to track down photo rights for his books. You opened a door that led me here.

To Mary D. Welch, who gave me my first editing project and showed me that publishing doesn't always require a giant company behind it – just passion and persistence.

To Alyson J. Bowels, who trusted me with my first official publishing project and saw her book purchased internationally. Your faith meant the world to me.

To my son, Brandon Siliezar: you're the reason I dared to think I could write a book at all. This might not be the story I imagined telling first—but you are my adventure buddy and my sunshine, always.

To the love of my life, David Perrin: thank you for seeing me at my highest, my lowest, and every messy moment in between. Thank you for believing in me even when I didn't believe in myself.

To my dad, Alex Siliezar: for all the wisdom you poured into me. "Loose lips sink ships," yes—but you also taught me that "a rising tide brings in all boats." Your words still guide me every day.

To my mom, Angela Siliezar, for the courage to choose a new path for both of us, and for giving me my dad. Thank you for teaching me that reinvention is always possible.

And finally, to every woman entrepreneur who has felt overwhelmed, underestimated, or unsure of where to start—this book is for you. May it remind you that your brilliance can never be boxed in.

Note on creation

This book was created from my soul, with strategy - and yes, a little bit of tech.

Throughout the writing process, I used AI-assisted tools to help me organize complex ideas, smooth transitions, and enhance clarity across chapters. But let's be clear: every concept, story, and insight you'll find here came from me - my lived experience, research, and years of supporting others.

The archetypes were developed in 2023 based on patterns I observed in myself and others. These archetypes became the foundation for a quiz, designed to help people understand how they show up in business and build stronger teams.

In 2025, I created the Energies of Brilliance™ - a framework that made those archetypes easier to discover, understand and apply. My goal was to group the archetypes into "departments," like in a well-run business, and show how different types contribute to success. AI helped me name the framework and pull it all together - but only because I trained it using my own voice, values, and thought process for years.

AI didn't replace my creativity or emotional intelligence - it simply helped me get what was in my head into your hands. It acted like a strategic assistant, allowing me to think faster, write more clearly, and build something more cohesive and transformational.

Just like I teach: the right tools won't dull your brilliance - they amplify it, so you can lead with less burnout and more clarity.

Glossary of Terms

Archetypes

Patterns of traits and behaviors that describe how you naturally show up in business. Think of them like your "go-to style" for leading, creating, connecting, or executing.

Energies of Brilliance™

The five core categories that group similar archetypes together, based on how your strengths flow:

- Creativity & Future-Orientation
- Structure & Implementation
- Strategy & Foresight
- Relationships & Communication
- Leadership & Support

Executive Dysfunction

A common challenge with planning, focus, motivation, or follow-through - even when you're passionate about the work. Often triggered by stress, overwhelm, or burnout.

Secondary Archetype

The second-strongest archetype within your **Primary Energy**. It adds dimension to how you operate day to day and shows up in different roles, moods, or seasons.

Secondary Energy

A different **Energy of Brilliance™** that also ranks high for you. It can become more active during stress, growth, or collaboration, offering unique flexibility in how you shine.

Dream Team

A group of people with complementary archetypes and energies - who balance each other's blind spots, reduce burnout, and get things done with more flow and less friction.

Least Compatible Archetype

The archetype whose natural style may clash with yours. It's not a dealbreaker - it just means extra communication, patience, or boundary-setting may be needed to thrive together.

From My Journey to Yours

Welcome, brilliant entrepreneur - yes, I mean you.

If you're holding this book, chances are you're a woman with big dreams and maybe a few tabs open in your brain at all times. You're ambitious, creative, and full of ideas… but also juggling overwhelm, uncertainty, or that quiet inner whisper asking, *"Am I doing this right?"*

I want you to know something: you're exactly where you need to be.

My journey into entrepreneurship didn't begin because I always wanted to run my own business. It began because I've always been curious. I wanted to know how things worked - and how to make them work better. I learned that not from textbooks, but from life, from my dad, and from growing up with a computer in the house before the internet even hit most schools.

When I was nineteen, I worked as an Executive Assistant to the General Manager of the Riverside Marriott, back when it was still the Holiday Inn under Sunstone Hotels. Before the end of my first year, Sunstone Hotels eliminated the Executive Assistant role entirely across all properties. But my General Manager didn't want to lose me, so he offered me an incredible opportunity: I could choose my own title and responsibilities, as long as I split my hours between departments.

So, I dove in. and over the years I worked Front Desk, Sales, Human Resources, Purchasing, Marketing, and even Food and Beverage development - including creating the Cobalt Club, a loyalty program for our restaurant, mostly because Mayor Loveridge (the City of Riverside's mayor) dined there every week at his specific table. Basically, I did everything except housekeeping, engineering, or the kitchen.

That experience opened my eyes to how many ways there are to run a business - and how thrilling it felt to connect the dots between them all. I think that's when the seed was planted that I wanted to do it all. And if I'm being honest, I've always felt a bit like that: part strategist, part artist, part system whisperer.

My dad was the one who taught me the concept of being "sandboxed." To him, it meant never boxing yourself in. He believed you should always look for ways to grow, stretch, and build new skills - to take the opportunities you're given, or create them yourself. He was an Engineering Project Manager at Motorola for thirty years, and from him, I learned not just how to think strategically, but how to show up for people, how to ask better questions, and how to trust the long game.

Years later, in my thirties, I had the chance to work on an international consulting project. It was exhilarating. I was diving into research, solving real-world business problems, and feeling like I'd cracked open a whole new part of my brain. I remember discovering The Boston Consulting Group and thinking, *Wow - these people get paid to solve puzzles all day? Sign me up!*

Spoiler alert: they did not sign me up. (Not for lack of trying - I applied a lot.)

But life had other plans. Eventually, I landed at a start-up consulting firm, and for the first time, I felt like I had my dream job. I was helping build the business from the ground up - researching everything from how to set up a 401(k) to opening a corporate rental car account. It was fast-paced, ever-changing, and oddly perfect for my brain that doesn't always work in straight lines.

And somewhere in all that hustle, the thought hit me:
"Why not start my own business?"

I didn't have all the answers. Heck, I didn't even have all the questions yet. But I knew one thing: getting started was the first step. And I've never been afraid of that first step, thanks to my dad - who taught me that life's too short to let yourself be pigeonholed.

Losing him in 2022 wrecked me. But his wisdom echoes in every part of who I am and what I've built. His voice still coaches me, still reminds me to check my energy, honor my purpose, and trust that if I'm doing work that fills me up instead of draining me, I'm on the right path.

So let me say this: if you're feeling stuck, unmotivated, or like your spark has dimmed, remember - sometimes you're not stuck. You're just *resting to launch*.

That's why I wrote this book - and why I founded Mariposa Sources.

When I first dreamed up Mariposa Sources, I created the tagline "your source for all services." But my dad's voice rang in my ears: that was way too vague. I didn't want to limit myself to just one thing - because I was still learning, experimenting, and figuring out how to work smarter, not harder. I wanted to build a business where I could get paid for being me - for doing the things I love, that come naturally, and that I could often do faster than most people because I'm always asking: *Can this be automated? Streamlined? Simplified?*

Of course, that's not how you start a business - and I learned that the hard way.

My first client was a bride, because I'd loved helping brides at the Riverside Marriott. But wedding planning was a lot of emotional and physical labor for one person. I gave being a travel agent a try, because I love travel, finding great deals, and my grandmother had her own travel agency in the 1980's. But then COVID hit - and suddenly, nobody was going *anywhere*.

So, I leaned into my Executive Assistant experience and became a virtual assistant, which I loved. I got to work on projects, learn new systems, and discover new ways to make businesses run more smoothly. But over time, I realized I didn't want to *do* the tasks anymore. I wanted to teach people how to do them for themselves. I wanted to empower, not just execute.

That led me to coaching and consulting. building workshops, memberships, and tools that could help others *decode their own brilliance.*

Mariposa Sources became my way of bringing all those threads together. It's your source for tools, insight, and inspiration to help you work smarter - not harder - and build a business (and life) that allows you to be fully, unapologetically *you.*

Whether it's through coaching, programs, resources, or digital systems, my mission is to help you step into your brilliance and make it shine.

Understanding who you are, and how you're wired to work, is the key to building a business that feels as good as it looks. Your quirks and unique strengths aren't obstacles; they're your *superpowers*.

Inside these pages, we're going to explore the Energies of Brilliance™ and the entrepreneurial archetypes that shape how you lead, build, and thrive. You'll discover why you do what you do, how to work with your energy (instead of against it), and how to find your place in the entrepreneurial ecosystem.

Because business isn't just about the work you do - it's about *who you become along the way*.

Let's take a deep breath. Settle in. And get ready to discover just how brilliant you already are.

A rising tide lifts all boats - and your tide is coming in.

Table of Contents

Understanding the Archetypes in Business

If there's one thing I've learned from working across hospitality, higher ed, government, small business, and consulting - it's this: business is never *just* business. It's personal.

Who we are shows up in everything we do. Our quirks, strengths, lived experience, and even our not-so-glamorous coping strategies shape the way we lead, create, sell, and serve. And for entrepreneurs, especially women juggling multiple roles and relationships, **self-awareness isn't just a "nice-to-have." It's your secret weapon.**

Because here's the truth: you can be brilliant, talented, and driven…
But if you're trying to run your business in a way that doesn't fit how you're wired, it will feel like you're pushing a boulder uphill.

Decisions feel heavier. Confidence takes longer to access. You start wondering if maybe *you're* the problem.

You're not.
You're the puzzle piece that was never meant to look like everyone else.

I've seen this play out in every type of client - brilliant women who were stuck not because they weren't capable, but because they were trying to copy someone else's way of doing things. **The difference between surviving and thriving often comes down to how well you know yourself - and how willing you are to honor your energy.**

For so many of us, the hardest part isn't the work itself. It's the constant internal tug-of-war between doing what *works for us* versus doing what we've been *told* we should do.

We ask ourselves questions like:

- How do I build a team that actually works well together?
- Who do I need - and who do I not need?
- How do I stop burning myself out doing things I'm not even good at?

These questions can keep us up at night because we're trying to build the big picture without fully understanding what pieces we're working with.

I've always had a knack for seeing both the big picture and the little inefficiencies others don't notice. But it wasn't until I started managing my own teams - and my own nervous system - that I realized how much *people* shape the flow of everything.

At first, I was obsessed with systems. (Okay, I still am.)

When I worked at the University of Redlands, one of my tasks was processing independent study contracts. It was this clunky process: three paper copies mailed back and forth between me, the student, and the instructor. It took 30 days and gave me a headache every single time.

I thought: If people can buy a house with an e-signature, why can't we enroll a student digitally?

I built a digital workflow that brought the timeline down from 30 days to ONE DAY. Suddenly, financial aid was processed faster, the Registrar's office wasn't behind, and students got what they needed *without the bottleneck.*

That moment showed me something I've never forgotten:

Systems are powerful - but the *people running them* are even more powerful.

And that's where archetypes come in.

Your archetype - along with your broader Energy of Brilliance™ - affects how you:

- **Handle tasks**: Do you thrive on structure or wait for inspiration to strike?
- **Build your team**: Are you energized by collaboration or drained by constant management?
- **Market yourself**: Are you the visionary who paints big pictures or the storyteller who weaves meaning?
- **Make decisions**: Do you rely on data or instinct? Planning or action?

When you understand your archetype, you stop squeezing yourself into someone else's template. You start moving in alignment with your own rhythm - and things flow better. You make faster decisions, you delegate without guilt, and you start building a business that feels sustainable *and* successful.

That's why I wrote this book. And that's why I never let go of Mariposa Sources.

Because I believe your brilliance is not something you need to find - it's something you need to *remember*. It's been there all along. And when you work in a way that reflects your natural energy, your business starts to feel like it fits you - instead of draining you.

This book isn't about labeling you or boxing you in.

It's a mirror to help you see yourself more clearly - and a roadmap to help you thrive.

Inside, you'll discover:

- How to harness your natural strengths (and avoid burnout from trying to "push through")
- How to spot and celebrate the strengths in others - so your team feels like magic, not mess
- Practical ways to run your business that honor your energy, not just your calendar
- And the confidence to stop playing small and start building what only *you* can build

Whether you're a Visionary dreaming up what's next, an Organizer calming the chaos, or a Peacemaker keeping harmony at the center of everything - this book is for you.

Let's unlock your archetype magic.

Let's work smarter, not harder.

And let's build a business - and a life - that feels as aligned on the inside as it looks on the outside.

The Five Energies of Brilliance™

Each of us has a core way we shine - how we work, lead, create, connect, and move through challenges. I call these the **Five Energies of Brilliance™**, and they're your keys to working in *flow*, not *friction*.

These Energies aren't about putting you in a box. They're about unlocking the box you've been stuck in.

Instead of forcing yourself to follow someone else's formula, you'll learn how to recognize your **natural strengths**, avoid burning out, and build a life and business that actually *fit* who you are.

Here's a quick preview of the five Energies of Brilliance™:

- **Creativity & Future-Orientation** – Visionary, imaginative, and full of fresh ideas
- **Structure & Implementation** – Grounded, practical, and focused on getting things done
- **Strategy & Foresight** – Analytical, big-picture, and always thinking five steps ahead
- **Relationships & Communication** – Empathetic, intuitive, and deeply connected to people
- **Leadership & Support** – Wise, nurturing, and committed to guiding others with integrity

Each Energy includes its own set of archetypes - think of them like your business personality styles. As you move through this book, you'll discover your **primary** and **secondary** strengths, how they interact, and how to use them to make aligned decisions, lead confidently, and create with ease.

You're not "too much." You're not "all over the place."

You're brilliant. And this is the roadmap to help you see it more clearly.

The Spark of Innovation: Creativity & Future-Orientation

"Where Bold Ideas Shape Tomorrow's Success"

Ever had a lightning-bolt idea hit you at the most random moment - shower, stoplight, or 2AM? Maybe it's not just one spark, but a whole *wildfire* of ideas crackling in your brain at once. That's the Creativity & Future-Orientation Energy of Brilliance™ - the part of you that sees what *could be*, even before it exists.

You don't need to be a painter, an app developer, or the next Elon Musk to be creative. If you've ever found yourself dreaming up new ways to serve people, solve problems, or shape the future, this energy is already alive in you.

And here's the truth: your ideas don't have to make sense to everyone. They just have to matter to *you* - and connect with the right people who are ready to build brilliance with you.

Why This Energy of Brilliance™ Matters

We live in a world where standing still means getting left behind. Innovation isn't a luxury anymore - it's how we adapt, grow, and lead.

If this Energy speaks to you, you're probably a Visionary, an Innovator, a Creative Catalyst - the kind of person who sees around corners and asks *Why not?*

You bring:

- Fresh offers that meet real (and unspoken) needs
- Messaging that stands out - not because it's loud, but because it's *true*
- Models and methods that challenge the status quo
- Energy that magnetizes the right people to your movement

Without you, business becomes a rinse-and-repeat cycle. But with your Energy in the mix? You turn possibility into momentum.

The Real Power in Action

This isn't just some abstract vibe. This Energy shows up in *real* decisions and *everyday leadership*.

When I worked at the University of Redlands, we had brilliant speakers visit campus - but the School of Business students were working adults that attended classes at the satellite campuses couldn't attend, due to timing and location. The lectures were valuable… but inaccessible.

In 2011, before livestreaming was a thing, I figured out how to rig Google Hangouts to broadcast the events to multiple campuses. Only a few years later, the University streamed graduation into air-conditioned classrooms, so family members didn't have to sit in the heat. That's future thinking. That's *seeing a gap and asking better questions*.

Your version of that moment might look different. Maybe it's spotting a client struggling and whipping up a checklist, a new intake flow, or a better way to explain a process. It doesn't have to be high-tech - it just has to work better than what came before.

When this Energy flows through you, you:

- Spot needs before others do
- Turn friction into inspiration
- Create things people didn't even know they were waiting for

Strengths & Challenges

What You Do Brilliantly:

- Dream up ideas others can't even imagine
- Adapt quickly when plans change
- Lead with inspiration and passion

What Might Trip You Up:

- Drowning in idea overload
- Struggling to delegate or trust others with your vision
- Waiting for perfection instead of hitting "publish"

Here's your permission slip, **done is often better than perfect.** Don't let a masterpiece die in your drafts folder. Your job isn't to finish the whole thing alone. It's to get it started, get it out, and let it grow.

Tips to Thrive in This Energy

- **Choose your sparks wisely.** Not every idea needs to become a project right now.

- **Surround yourself with "finishers."** Find partners who love completing what you start.
- **Start messy.** Try the idea. Test the offer. Let it evolve. Clarity comes through motion.

Your Superpower

If this Energy lights you up, you're not just creative - you're *brilliantly* future-minded. You see possibilities like others see problems.

You're not here to wait for permission. You're here to *set trends, lead change, and create ripple effects.*

Trust the spark. Nurture it.
And remember: the world doesn't need another cookie-cutter brand.
It needs *your* vision - loud, messy, and wildly magnetic.

If this Energy of Brilliance™ resonates with you, know this:
You're not too much.
You're not scattered.
You're a visionary with a mission - and the world is ready for what only *you* can imagine into being.

Building Foundations: Structure & Implementation

"Where Vision Becomes Reality, One Step at a Time"

Let's get real: brilliant ideas are powerful - but without a plan, they stay locked in journals, lost in voice memos, or trapped in your Notes app under "someday." That's where the Structure & Implementation Energy of Brilliance™ steps in.

This is the energy of the Builders, the Finishers, the Quiet Powerhouses who ask, "Okay, how are we actually going to make this happen?" You're the one who brings the magic down to Earth - one system, checklist, and process at a time.

Maybe you love your color-coded planner like it's a second brain. Maybe you get a rush from tightening up timelines or solving logistical puzzles like it's a game. Or maybe you've resisted structure because it felt limiting... until you realized that the *right* structure sets you free.

If this Energy speaks to you, you're not "just organized." You're the *backbone* of brilliance. And that's a creative gift, too.

Why This Energy of Brilliance™ Matters

Ideas light the spark, but execution builds the fire. And businesses don't thrive on sparks alone - they thrive on follow-through.

While visionaries imagine the future, it's the Builders who lay the bricks, set the timeline, and make sure no one forgets the budget. Without structure, chaos creeps in. Without implementation, even the most beautiful strategy collects dust.

This Energy matters because:

- You transform chaos into calm
- You create systems that support creativity - not suppress it
- You keep things on time, on track, and on purpose
- You turn the *what if* into *what's next*

Most importantly? **Your structure creates space.** For creativity, for rest, for growth that *doesn't burn you out*.

The Real Power in Action

This isn't about rules or being the "no-fun" person in the room. It's about helping the vision actually *happen*.

Way back - pre-Instagram, pre-app culture - I was designing a loyalty program for the Riverside Marriott's hotel restaurant. But it wasn't just a "cool idea." I mapped out the enrollment, the tracking, the messaging, and the team training. I didn't just build the promo - I built the *infrastructure*. That's Structure Energy in action: building something that works *with or without you*.

Or picture this:
Someone says, "Let's do a fun team escape room!"
And immediately, your brain goes:

- What's the budget?
- Who's staying to cover the phones?
- Can we get a group discount?
- What's the plan for dietary needs?

You're not a buzzkill. You're the reason fun *actually happens*. That's your magic.

Strengths & Challenges

What You Do Brilliantly:

- Turn big ideas into actionable steps
- Spot obstacles before they turn into fires
- Keep people, plans, and systems in sync
- Create clarity and calm for the whole team

Where You Might Struggle:

- Feeling like the "task person" instead of a visionary
- Getting caught in prep and never launching
- Believing structure isn't creative (it is!)
- Struggling to trust others to follow through like you do

Here's your reminder: **structure *is* strategy.** And strategy is sacred.

Tips to Thrive in This Energy

- **Balance planning with action.** A beautiful plan only works if it's in motion.

- **Keep it simple.** Complicated systems don't equal better ones - ease is the goal.
- **Plan for *real* life.** Budget in time, energy, and the occasional curveball.
- **Celebrate tiny wins.** A checked box is a confidence boost in disguise.
- **Progress over perfection.** Launch. Learn. Repeat. That's how momentum builds.

Your Superpower

You're the bridge between dreams and done.

You bring order to chaos. Vision to life.

And your calm, grounded energy is the reason people trust the process - and each other.

So no, you're not "just organized." You are *essential.*

You are the reason timelines don't crumble, projects don't stall, and dreams don't stay buried in Google Docs.

When you lean into this Energy, you become the *foundation* brilliance is built on.

And that? That's what makes everything else *possible.*

If this Energy of Brilliance™ resonates with you, know this:

You're not boring.

You're not background.

You're the backbone of brilliance - and your quiet power is what makes big things possible.

The Architects of Insight: Strategy & Foresight

"Where Clarity and Strategy Shape Lasting Success"

Some people leap into action.

Others pause, read the map - and sometimes redraw it from scratch.

That's the magic of the Strategy & Foresight Energy of Brilliance™.

If this Energy resonates with you, you're the architect. The one who sees what's coming before the rest of the room even knows it's a conversation worth having. You think in steps, patterns, and ripple effects. You ask better questions - not because you're stalling, but because you're *building something that lasts.*

Maybe you're the spreadsheet whisperer, the person who reads the fine print, the quiet storm in the Zoom room who drops the one question that shifts everything. You don't just plan - you *design with purpose.*

And while you sometimes wish you could "just do the thing" like others, you know there's power in *thinking before moving.* That's not hesitation - it's strategy. And it's brilliant.

Why This Energy of Brilliance™ Matters

In a world that glorifies hustle and gut-check decisions, Strategy & Foresight is the steady breath in the chaos.

This Energy is what protects businesses from falling into shiny-object syndrome, burnout cycles, and costly mistakes. You're not the loudest voice - but you're often the wisest one in the room.

You bring:

- Clarity in the clutter
- Long-term thinking in a short-term world
- Risk reduction through smart design
- Stability that helps teams feel safe, prepared, and confident

Without you, people act fast - but often without direction. With you? They move smarter, more sustainably, and with *purpose*.

The Real Power in Action

This Energy shows up in subtle, often behind-the-scenes brilliance.

When I worked at the San Bernardino International Airport, I noticed we were bleeding money on copier costs - like thousands a year. While most people shrugged and said, "that's just the contract," I asked better questions. I dug through invoices, built a cost model, analyzed supply usage, and found a smarter way forward. My spreadsheet shaved $10,000 a year off the budget. No fanfare. Just smart, strategic insight that made a real difference.

That's the Strategy & Foresight Energy:
Spot the pattern. Reroute the problem. Design the better way.

Maybe for you, it shows up as a checklist that prevents project creep, a habit of looking at data *before* a launch, or a natural instinct to slow down and ask, *"But what happens after this?"*

You're not being negative. You're laying down the safety net that lets others leap.

That's not overthinking. That's leadership.

Strengths & Challenges

What You Do Brilliantly:

- See connections others miss
- Turn chaos into clear plans
- Solve problems before they spiral
- Make businesses smarter, leaner, and more resilient

Where You Might Struggle:

- Overthinking every possible outcome
- Struggling to let go and let others execute your vision
- Feeling "too slow" in a fast-paced environment
- Questioning if you're creative "enough"

Let's clear this up now:

Strategy *is* creativity.

You're just using your brain to architect better outcomes instead of painting pictures. That *is* art.

Tips to Thrive in This Energy

- **Time-box your thinking process.** Give yourself a research window, then take action - even if it's a small step.

- **Break big plans down.** Clarity comes faster when you take your brilliance out of your head and onto the page.

- **Partner with activators.** You bring the "how," they bring the "go." Together? You're unstoppable.

- **Own your value.** You save time, money, and stress before others even see the risk. That's magic.

- **Start before it's perfect.** Even the smartest plan needs motion to matter.

Your Superpower

You are the architect.

The strategist.

The quiet force that sees the endgame while others are still playing checkers.

You're the one who can take a swirling mess of ideas and turn them into a roadmap, a budget, or a launch plan that actually makes sense. You connect today's actions to tomorrow's outcomes - and that is no small thing.

So don't shrink. Don't second-guess.

Your insight is what keeps businesses sustainable, people empowered, and visions alive.

If this Energy of Brilliance™ calls to you, own it.

You're not slow - you're strategic.

You're not too careful - you're *crafted*.

And you're not just planning for success...

You're building it.

The Heart of Business: Relationships & Communication

"Where Human Connection Fuels Business Growth"

Systems are important. Products have power.

But *people*? They're the true heartbeat of your business.

The Relationships & Communication Energy of Brilliance™ belongs to the connectors, the peacemakers, and the natural communicators who turn conversations into community. If this is your Energy, you're the person everyone feels safe around. The one who holds space for hard truths, big dreams, and everything in between.

You may have been told that you're "too sensitive" or "not business-minded enough" - but let's be clear: you're the reason businesses don't just *function…* they *flourish*.

Why This Energy of Brilliance™ Matters

We're living in a connection economy. People don't just buy what you offer - they buy how you make them *feel*.

This Energy of Brilliance™ matters because:

- Clients want to feel seen, heard, and understood
- Teams work better when trust is at the center
- Collaborations thrive when communication is honest and clear

- Conflict dissolves when people feel safe to speak up

You, dear empath, are the translator of feelings, the bridge between people and possibility. You help by:

- Turning customers into loyal fans
- Turning strangers into collaborators
- Turn misunderstandings into growth moments

Your presence doesn't just open doors - it keeps them open.

The Real Power in Action

Relationship magic doesn't mean being "talkative" or "nice." It means *intentional connection.*

Like the time I partnered with a micro-influencer. I poured energy into the collaboration but didn't ask what I needed in return. The vibe was great, but there was no structure to sustain it. That taught me: *even the most genuine connection needs clarity to thrive.*

Or the time I ran a webinar series and sent thank-you emails - even to those who didn't attend. One woman booked a 15-minute call, which turned into a two-hour heart-to-heart. She joined my program not because I pitched her… but because she *felt seen.*

But here's the catch: empathy without boundaries can backfire. She wasn't ready for the program, she just needed coaching, and I hadn't clarified expectations. It rippled into my launch plans and reminded me:

Connection needs direction.

Otherwise, we give everything and get left empty.

That's the lesson of this Energy: care deeply, but don't forget to lead. Relationships move business - but *you* get to set the pace.

Strengths & Challenges

What You Do Brilliantly:

- Build trust quickly and naturally
- Read the energy in a room (or DM thread) like a pro
- Make people feel seen, safe, and supported
- Turn everyday interactions into meaningful connections

Where You Might Struggle:

- Saying yes too often to protect people's feelings
- Holding back on selling because it feels "pushy"
- Leaving out your offers in conversations that *could* convert
- Feeling drained from giving more than you receive

Let's reframe this:

Your sensitivity is *strength*.

Your voice isn't "too much" - it's *exactly what someone needs to hear.*

Tips to Thrive in This Energy

- **Connect with clarity.** Know what you want from a relationship - and communicate it early with love.

- **Build gentle boundaries.** You can be kind *and* protect your energy. It's not selfish - it's sustainable.
- **Practice asking.** Whether it's a call-to-action or a collaboration ask, people *want* to support you. Let them.
- **Check your capacity.** You don't need to show up everywhere. Just show up fully where it matters.
- **Validate your worth.** Your emotional labor is valuable. Your presence *is* a business asset.

Your Superpower

You are the pulse.

The human touch in the automated inbox.

The voice that reminds people they matter - not just as clients, but as whole humans.

You build loyalty that no ad campaign can buy.

You hold space for transformation.

And you lead with love - not instead of leadership, but *as* leadership.

So, if this Energy of Brilliance™ resonates with you, know this:

You're not too much.

You're not too soft.

You're *exactly what this world - and this business landscape - needs.*

Your gift isn't just connection.

It's connection with *intention.* And that's where the magic lives.

The Guiding Light: Leadership & Support

"Where Wisdom and Care Illuminate the Path to Success"

Business isn't just numbers and strategy - it's people trying to figure life out in real time. Its courage wrapped in self-doubt, ambition held back by imposter syndrome, and dreams shaped by lived experience.

And sometimes, what we need most isn't a business plan.
We need someone who's walked the path ahead and is willing to shine a light behind them.

That's the heart of the Leadership & Support Energy of Brilliance™.

If this is your Energy, you're a steady presence. A truth-teller with a soft touch. The one people call at 11 p.m. because they know you won't just give advice - you'll listen, hold space, and remind them who they are.

You don't just see people as they are - you see *who they're becoming.*
And even when you carry your own doubts, you still find the strength to say, "You've got this."

Why This Energy of Brilliance™ Matters

Let's be honest - business is hard.
There are moments that shake us:

- Late-night anxiety spirals

- Big decisions with no clear answers
- Burnout that sneaks in under the guise of "just one more thing"
- Feeling isolated, even when surrounded by others

In those moments, we don't need gurus. We need *guides*.

People who bring not just experience, but compassion.

People who don't just point to the map - they walk it *with* us.

This Energy of Brilliance™ matters because:

- People stay loyal when they feel safe and seen
- Teams evolve under mentorship, not micromanagement
- Wisdom steadies the ship when the storm rolls in
- Cultures flourish when leadership is grounded in *care*

You're not just building businesses - you're building people. And that changes *everything*.

The Real Power in Action

If you resonate with this Energy, you've likely been the "go-to" person since forever.

You're the group chat counselor. The one your friends - and clients - turn to when life gets real.

I've been there, too.

Once, a client I adored became more of a friend... and suddenly our paid sessions blurred into free advice, long texts, and unspoken expectations. I kept showing up, but I was *drained*. It wasn't her fault - I hadn't set boundaries. And it hit me:

Charging for your guidance isn't selfish. It's sacred.

It honors the energy, wisdom, and space you hold.

This Energy is powerful because it offers transformation.
Not through control - but through compassion.
Not by fixing people - but by helping them remember they can rise.

Strengths & Challenges

What You Do Brilliantly:

- Offer empathy with depth - not pity
- See potential in people long before they do
- Supporting others without ego
- Provide wisdom that's lived, not just learned
- Build deep, unshakable trust

Where You Might Struggle:

- Feeling like you're "always on" for others
- Carrying guilt around charging for your support
- Feeling frustrated when people don't follow your advice
- Taking on the emotional weight of others' outcomes
- Wondering if you're "expert enough" to lead

Let me tell you this:

Leadership isn't about being perfect.

It's about being present. Consistent. Courageous. You already are.

Tips to Thrive in This Energy

- **Honor your capacity.** You're not a 24/7 hotline. Set boundaries that let you *stay available* without being *exhausted*.

- **Charge without apology.** What you offer is more than advice - it's transformation. And that has value.

- **Let go of the outcome.** Support doesn't mean control. People grow on their own timeline.

- **Balance presence with action.** Sometimes, people need a nudge - not just a hug.

- **Nurture yourself first.** You *can't* pour from an empty cup - your brilliance deserves care, too.

Your Superpower

You are the warm light in a hard moment.

The quiet coach in someone's breakthrough.

The mirror that reflects a version of others they're still growing into.

You lead with heart. With integrity. With love that holds people accountable and lifts them higher.

So, if this Energy of Brilliance™ calls to you, own it.

You're not "just supportive." You're *transformative*.

You don't just manage people - you *believe* in them.

And that belief?

It's the kind that builds legacies.

Discover Your Energy of Brilliance™ Quiz

Instructions:

Read each statement below, and mark how strongly you agree or disagree. Go with your first instinct - there's no right or wrong answer!

Creativity & Future-Orientation

1. I often come up with ideas that challenge how things are usually done.

   Strongly Disagree

   Disagree

   Neutral

   Agree

   Strongly Agree

2. I'm energized by imagining how the future could be different.

   Strongly Disagree

   Disagree

   Neutral

   Agree

   Strongly Agree

3. I love starting new projects, even if I haven't finished the last one yet.

   Strongly Disagree

   Disagree

   Neutral

   Agree

   Strongly Agree

4. I see possibilities where others see problems.

   Strongly Disagree

   Disagree

   Neutral

   Agree

   Strongly Agree

Get your score for the Creativity & Future-Orientation Energy of Brilliance™: Add the points for questions tied to each question.

- Strongly Disagree (1)
- Disagree (2)
- Neutral (3)
- Agree (4)
- Strongly Agree (5)

Structure & Implementation

1. I feel comfortable when there's a clear plan or system to follow.

   Strongly Disagree

   Disagree

   Neutral

   Agree

   Strongly Agree

2. I like turning ideas into practical, step-by-step actions.

   Strongly Disagree

   Disagree

   Neutral

   Agree

   Strongly Agree

3. I enjoy organizing details to keep things running smoothly.

   Strongly Disagree

   Disagree

   Neutral

   Agree

   Strongly Agree

4. I prefer routine and consistency over constant change.

Strongly Disagree

Disagree

Neutral

Agree

Strongly Agree

Get your score for the Structure & Implementation Energy of Brilliance™: Add the points for questions tied to each question.

- Strongly Disagree (1)
- Disagree (2)
- Neutral (3)
- Agree (4)
- Strongly Agree (5)

Strategy & Foresight

1. I enjoy analyzing information to understand how things work.

    Strongly Disagree

    Disagree

    Neutral

    Agree

    Strongly Agree

2. I often think about how today's decisions will affect the future.

    Strongly Disagree

    Disagree

    Neutral

    Agree

    Strongly Agree

3. I prefer to become deeply skilled in one area rather than in many.

    Strongly Disagree

    Disagree

    Neutral

    Agree

    Strongly Agree

4. I like considering all possible outcomes before taking action.

Strongly Disagree

Disagree

Neutral

Agree

Strongly Agree

Get your score for the Strategy & Foresight Energy of Brilliance™: Add the points for questions tied to each question.

- Strongly Disagree (1)
- Disagree (2)
- Neutral (3)
- Agree (4)
- Strongly Agree (5)

Relationships & Communication

1. I naturally connect people who could help each other.

   Strongly Disagree

   Disagree

   Neutral

   Agree

   Strongly Agree

2. I feel energized when I'm working with or talking to others.

   Strongly Disagree

   Disagree

   Neutral

   Agree

   Strongly Agree

3. I'm good at resolving misunderstandings between people.

   Strongly Disagree

   Disagree

   Neutral

   Agree

   Strongly Agree

4. I love building relationships and expanding my network.

Strongly Disagree

Disagree

Neutral

Agree

Strongly Agree

Get your score for the Relationships & Communication Energy of Brilliance™: Add the points for questions tied to each question.

- Strongly Disagree (1)
- Disagree (2)
- Neutral (3)
- Agree (4)
- Strongly Agree (5)

Leadership & Support

1. People often come to me for advice or support.

   Strongly Disagree

   Disagree

   Neutral

   Agree

   Strongly Agree

2. I enjoy helping others grow and develop.

   Strongly Disagree

   Disagree

   Neutral

   Agree

   Strongly Agree

3. I feel fulfilled when I see someone succeed because of my guidance.

   Strongly Disagree

   Disagree

   Neutral

   Agree

   Strongly Agree

4. I believe sharing knowledge is key to a team's success.

   Strongly Disagree

   Disagree

   Neutral

   Agree

   Strongly Agree

Get your score for the Leadership & Support Energy of Brilliance™: Add the points for questions tied to each question.

- Strongly Disagree (1)
- Disagree (2)
- Neutral (3)
- Agree (4)
- Strongly Agree (5)

Scoring Instructions

Scoring each Energy of Brilliance™:

- Add the points for questions tied to each Energy of Brilliance™.
    - Strongly Disagree (1)
    - Disagree (2)
    - Neutral (3)
    - Agree (4)
    - Strongly Agree (5)

The Energy of Brilliance™ with the highest total = **Your Dominant Energy of Brilliance™.**

The next-highest = Your Secondary Energy of Brilliance™.

(Max score per Energy of Brilliance™: 20. Range: 4–20.)

Dive into Your Energy of Brilliance™

Creativity & Future-Orientation Energy

"Where bold ideas shape what's possible."

Welcome back, visionary.

If you're here, you're likely someone whose mind lights up with "What if?" moments. Not just sometimes - but all the time. You're the one scribbling notes during meetings, dreaming up new offers while brushing your teeth, and spotting trends before the rest of the world knows what's coming.

This is the Creativity & Future-Orientation Energy of Brilliance™ - and you're right at home here.

When I first started building the Energies of Brilliance™ framework, I thought I had it all figured out. I created a super-detailed quiz that would *surely* help people find their brilliance. I poured my creativity into it, mapped out every question, every outcome…

And then no one finished it.
Unless I personally walked them through it.

I could've scrapped the whole thing, but instead, I zoomed out. I got curious. I started asking *better* questions - just like I always have. And that's when it hit me: the magic isn't in the perfect system. It's in the invitation to see yourself differently.

That's what this Energy is all about.
You don't wait for the future - you *create* it.

Why This Energy of Brilliance™ Is So Powerful

People with this Energy are the spark. The ones asking *why not?* while everyone else is still wondering *how?* You're the kind of thinker who connects dots others don't even see. You inspire people, challenge the norm, and breathe life into what's next.

And yet…

Sometimes it feels like your mind won't stop.

Sometimes you feel like you're ten steps ahead of everyone.

Sometimes you wonder if you're too much - or not "organized enough."

Let me be clear:

You're not scattered.

You're not "too out there."

You're not behind because you have ten ideas in your Notes app and haven't picked one yet.

You're brilliant. And this chapter is about helping you *own that brilliance without burning out.*

How This Energy Might Show Up For You

You may be someone who:

- **Spots possibilities** where others see limitations
- **Craves variety**, inspiration, and innovation
- **Feels restless** in highly structured or repetitive roles
- **Lights up** during brainstorming or big-picture visioning

- **Feels a little lonely** because your ideas are bigger than your current circle can hold

Sound familiar? If you're nodding, take a breath. You're not alone - and you're exactly where you're meant to be.

Your Brilliance in Action

At your best, you:

- **Connect ideas** across industries and experiences
- **Inspire people** with your forward-thinking energy
- **Lead with curiosity**, wonder, and a hunger for growth
- **Spot trends** before they hit mainstream
- **Bring momentum** and excitement into every room you enter

Your ideas aren't distractions.

They're *downloads*.

They're your blueprint for shaping what's next.

What Fuels Your Energy

You're at your best when you have:

- Freedom to pivot and experiment
- Brainstorming sessions without judgment
- Time to dream - without immediate pressure to produce
- Collaborative spaces with other creatives
- Tools that help capture and organize sparks of inspiration

What Might Drain You

- Repetitive tasks with no room for creativity
- Being told to "stay in your lane"
- Endless processes that stall momentum
- Hearing "that'll never work" one too many times
- Idea overload with no outlet or structure

Sometimes, when your brain is on overdrive, you'll crave doing mindless things just to turn it off. That's not you being lazy. That's your creativity calling for a *reset*.

Your Strengths

- Original thinking
- Visionary insights
- Challenging the status quo
- Courage to dream big
- Ability to adapt in fast-moving spaces

Your Growth Opportunities

- Prioritizing which ideas to focus on
- Overextending your mental bandwidth
- Feeling misunderstood or dismissed
- Avoiding follow-through or details
- Losing steam once the novelty wears off

These aren't flaws. They're signs that you need systems that *support* your Energy - not suppress it.

Thriving in This Energy (a.k.a. Your Magic Sauce)

- **Focus on 1 or 2 ideas at a time.** Let the rest wait - document them for later.

- **Partner with people who *love* structure.** Think: finishers, organizers, implementers.

- **Build in rest time.** Creativity isn't sustainable when you're running on fumes.

- **Don't try to explain everything.** Share the *vision,* not every detail. Let others see the spark.

- **Celebrate your wins.** Especially the ones that didn't exist last year - because you created them.

Business Tips for Creative Trailblazers

- Pair your brilliance with consistent support - like templates, automation, or a strategic Virtual Assistant.

- Stay open to refining ideas instead of tossing them when they get messy.

- Invite others into your vision with *clarity* - so they can catch the spark and run with you.

- Track your "idea vault" (Notion, Google Doc, voice memos - whatever works). It keeps inspiration organized, not overwhelming.

Remember: your gift isn't just in seeing what's next. It's believing in it - and building a path others can walk, too.

Ready to Go Deeper?

You've tapped into your Creativity & Future-Orientation Energy. Now it's time to discover your **specific archetype** - your unique lens for how this brilliance shows up in your work, your leadership, and your business style.

Turn the page to take the quiz.

Let's *decode* the way you shine.

Discover Your Archetype Quiz

Instructions: Read each statement below and choose the one that sounds most like you. Don't overthink it - go with your gut!

---

1. When inspiration strikes, you:

A) Immediately share the idea and rally others around it.

B) Dive into the idea, experimenting and exploring possibilities.

C) Think about how this idea fits into a bigger, future vision.

---

2. People often describe you as:

A) Energetic and full of contagious enthusiasm.

B) Original and inventive, always trying new things.

C) Visionary and able to see what others can't.

---

3. Your favorite part of launching something new is:

A) Getting others excited and pushing it into action quickly.

B) Playing with creative ways to bring it to life.

C) Knowing it will make a big impact on the future.

---

4. When facing a challenge, you:

A) Jump in, ready to shake things up fast.

B) Look for innovative solutions no one's tried yet.

C) Step back and consider how this affects the long-term vision.

---

5. Your biggest motivation in business is:

A) Sparking momentum and inspiring fast progress.

B) Exploring fresh ideas and breaking out of routine.

C) Leaving a lasting legacy and changing the world.

---

6. Your creative energy feels:

A) Like a spark that sets others in motion.

B) Like an endless well of new concepts and experiments.

C) Like a guiding light toward a bigger future.

Scoring

Mostly A's → You're The Catalyst

Mostly B's → You're The Innovator

Mostly C's → You're The Visionary

Archetypes in This Energy of Brilliance™

The Catalyst

Welcome to the world of fireworks, fast lanes, and fearless momentum. The Catalyst is dynamic, energetic, and wired to create change. You're the spark that sets things in motion - often before anyone else has even finished their coffee. You don't wait for permission - you move. You're bold, intuitive, and you trust action as your compass.

Think of people like **Sara Blakely**, who turned frustration over visible panty lines into the billion-dollar brand Spanx, or **Richard Branson**, who built entire industries from scratch simply because he couldn't sit still. Catalysts don't just follow trends - they *create* them. They look at the status quo and say, "Cool story... now let's flip it on its head."

But your rapid-fire energy, while electric, can also leave scorched earth behind. Half-built ideas, overextended teams, or burnout can sneak in if you don't build as smart as you sprint. Your gift lies not just in starting - but in knowing what's truly worth finishing.

How to Spot a Catalyst

- Thinks in brainstorms, speaks in bursts, acts in brilliance.
- Has five browser tabs open - and five businesses half-built.
- Starts projects on impulse (and sometimes finishes them... later).
- Can feel bored by tradition, repetition, or caution.

- Needs space to create without being micromanaged.
- At your best when you're following your gut - not a rigid 10-step plan.

Strengths

- Sparks transformation and forward motion.
- Sees big potential and isn't afraid to chase it.
- Challenges the "we've always done it this way" mentality.
- Creates urgency that wakes people (and businesses) up.
- Energizes a room just by being in it.
- Moves from idea to action faster than most can make a to-do list.

Shadow Side

- Starts strong but fizzles fast when the excitement fades.
- Moves so quickly they forget to bring others along.
- Reacts on impulse - sometimes launching before the vision is clear.
- Gets frustrated by delays and derails progress with abrupt pivots.
- Can unintentionally exhaust others with their intensity and urgency.

Emotional Cost (Internal)

When out of alignment, Catalysts can feel:

- Boxed in by overplanning or too many approvals
- Misunderstood - like their speed is seen as recklessness
- Overstimulated by the pressure to always be "on"

- Frustrated when others hesitate, stall, or question the obvious
- Drained from constantly pulling others into action

Remember: Your gift is momentum, not martyrdom. Pause isn't punishment. Stillness gives your fire somewhere meaningful to burn.

Stress Triggers (External)

- Red tape, bureaucracy, or systems that require slow buy-in
- Teammates who delay decisions or resist change
- Lack of clarity or autonomy in fast-moving projects
- Overly structured environments that restrict innovation
- Being sidelined or dismissed as "too much" when proposing bold moves

Growth Tips (When to Ask for Help)

Catalyst, you are power in motion - but even power needs to be grounded. Ask yourself:

- Is this the right time… or just the most exciting?
- What support do I need to bring this idea to life sustainably?
- Am I honoring my energy cycles - or pushing through burnout?
- Who can help me finish what I start, so I don't abandon my own brilliance?

Remember: your speed is a gift when it's matched with support, pacing, and purpose.

Least Compatible (But Also Most Growth-Expanding)

Say hello to your favorite frenemy: The Analyst.

You're ready to leap. They're still building the parachute (and checking it for flaws). You thrive on bold, intuitive moves. They find peace in precision, patterns, and proof.

You might see them as slow, skeptical, or caught in analysis paralysis. They might see you as reckless, impulsive, or allergic to planning.

The truth? You need each other.

Your energy sparks movement. Their insight ensures that momentum leads somewhere worthwhile. When you team up with patience and mutual respect, magic happens. You don't need to dim your fire - just aim it with intention.

So next time you feel blocked, try this mantra:

"Momentum moves mountains. Data shows which ones to climb."

Dream Team Suggestions

You don't need clones - you need the right colleagues.
Your best team includes:

- **The Strategist** – They hold the long-term plan and help you tie your flash of genius to something sustainable.
- **The Organizer** – Brings systems that support your energy instead of stifling it.
- **The Executor** – Gets sh*t done and keeps your visions from staying stuck in your Google Drive.

- **The Peacemaker** – Maintains harmony when your whirlwind pace shakes the team.
- **The Innovator** – Matches your energy and brings even more creative fire to the brainstorm table.

Bottom Line: Together, this team makes sure your sparks become flames… without burning the house down.

Business Wisdom for the Catalyst

You don't need a blueprint - you need a runway.

Start with your vision and surround yourself with people who help you build it with care.

Here's your brilliance-in-action alignment guide:

- Prioritize what you *finish* as much as what you start.
- Invest in systems that give your ideas structure.
- Let trusted partners slow you down - not to stop you, but to help you land safely.
- Celebrate progress, not just launch day.
- Communicate your "why" often - your team wants to run with you, not chase you.

☑ Own your role as a Catalyst. The world needs people willing to act boldly.

☑ Don't fear pacing - it's what keeps your fire sustainable.

☑ Keep charging ahead - but pause long enough to bring others with you.

Your gift is initiating change while others are still weighing the risk. You move ideas into action - and help the world move forward.

A note to you: Catalyst, you are brilliance in motion. A firestarter. A change agent. You move the needle when others are still stuck in doubt. But you don't need to hustle harder to prove your worth - you need support systems that honor your speed *and* protect your energy. Your spark is sacred. You were never meant to do it all alone. You're not too much. You're the momentum that makes the mission real. Let's make sure your fire fuels something lasting.

The Innovator

Welcome to the mind of the perpetual inventor, the idea factory, the person whose brain practically hums with *What if...?* energy. The Innovator is a creative problem-solver, brimming with originality, curiosity, and the courage to see beyond the obvious. You're the one who stares at an everyday annoyance and instantly starts mentally redesigning it from scratch.

You're in good company. Think **James Dyson**, who dismantled 5,127 prototypes to revolutionize the vacuum, or **Steve Jobs**, whose obsession with beauty, usability, and disruption changed the way we communicate, work, and listen to music. Innovators live in the liminal space between frustration and breakthrough - constantly sketching, dreaming, tweaking, testing.

But with all those ideas bouncing around, it's easy to scatter your brilliance or burn out from chasing too many sparks at once. Your magic? Turning possibility into progress - without losing your fire in the process.

How to Spot an Innovator

- Has seventeen tabs open - and they're all titled something like "BIG IDEA: Read Later."
- Doodles business models on receipts, napkins, or the back of parking tickets.

- Thinks "pivot" is just part of breakfast conversation.
- Gets visibly lit up when brainstorming - the vibe is *palpable*.
- Finds repetition draining (like, paint-drying-on-walls levels of boring).
- Is regularly told, "Whoa, that's… actually kinda brilliant."

Strengths

- Sees possibilities others miss.
- Turns problems into playful challenges.
- Sparks new directions and revitalizes stale strategies.
- Brings fresh energy and bold creativity to the team.
- Adapts quickly and thrives in change.
- Naturally sees the future - and how to shape it.

Shadow Side

- Can get stuck in idea overload without follow-through.
- Overestimates how fast or easy it is to execute a vision.
- Struggles to stay engaged in rigid or repetitive environments.
- Can unintentionally derail momentum with "just one more idea."
- Risks being misunderstood or dismissed as "unrealistic."

Emotional Cost (Internal)

When you're not in flow, your brilliance can feel like a burden. You might feel:

- Restless with too many ideas or options and no clear direction to channel them.

- Frustrated that others can't see the connections you see so clearly.
- Guilty for losing interest in what once excited you.
- Mentally scattered from trying to hold too many threads at once.
- Lonely, like your brain is always ten tabs ahead of everyone else.

Remember: Your creativity is a gift - not a to-do list. You don't need to act on every spark. You need space, stillness, and containers that help your brilliance take shape.

Stress Triggers (External)

- Rigid systems that demand linear thinking
- Feedback that focuses only on practicality, not possibility
- Micromanagement that stifles creative flow
- Being told to "stick to the plan" when a better idea arises
- Deadlines without flexibility for ideation or iteration

Growth Tips (When to Ask for Help)

You're not *just* an idea machine - you're a visionary leader. But even leaders need help turning sparks into strategies.

When things start feeling too scattered or heavy, ask:

- What's *really* lighting me up right now - and what can wait?
- Who can help ground this idea without dulling its shine?
- Have I explained my vision in a way others can act on it?
- What system would make follow-through feel easier (not heavier)?
- Am I chasing creativity… or avoiding discomfort?

Remember: You don't have to do it all. Your genius grows when it's supported.

Least Compatible (But Also Most Growth-Expanding)

Say hello to your favorite frenemy: The Implementer.

You're high concept. They're high consistency. While you're pitching your next disruptive idea, they're over there polishing the process that worked last year.

You might see them as rigid, unimaginative, or resistant to change. They might see you as scattered, chaotic, or unrealistic.

The truth? You *need* each other.

Your ideas are world-changing - but only if they're built on a solid foundation. Implementers help you make sure your magic *lands*.

So, breathe through the resistance, and try this mantra:

"A brilliant idea deserves a brilliant plan."

Dream Team Suggestions

Innovator, you are the focused on the future - but every future needs a reality.

Your best collaborators include:

- **The Executor** – Turns your brilliance into reality. They're the ones who say, "I've got this. Here's the timeline."

- **The Strategist** – Zooms out to make sure your ideas align with your bigger mission (and don't eat your whole budget).
- **The Organizer** – Keeps your work on track, your systems humming, and your inbox from imploding.
- **The Analyst** – Brings grounded insight to test your ideas before they launch. Data = your safety net.
- **The Mentor** – Offers perspective and grounding, helping you refine ideas without clipping your wings.

Bottom Line: You spark the future. They help it take shape.

Business Wisdom for the Innovator

Your magic isn't just ideas - it's transformation. But even the most dazzling idea needs structure to become sustainable.

Here's your brilliance-in-action alignment guide:

- Prioritize one idea at a time - and protect it until it launches.
- Co-create with people who love execution as much as you love imagination.
- Don't get stuck waiting for perfection. Launch messy, refine later.
- Learn to share your vision in a way that others can see and support.
- Let your systems be scaffolding - not cages - for your creativity.

☑ Own your role as an Innovator. The world desperately needs new ideas.

☑ Don't fear feedback - it's how your brilliance reaches more people.

☑ Keep dreaming boldly - but ground those dreams in action.

Your gift is turning curiosity into invention. You don't just imagine better - you dare to build it.

A note to you: Innovator, you're the future in human form. Your curiosity is contagious. Your originality is the antidote to mediocrity. You spark what others can't even name yet. But your ideas aren't meant to live only in your mind. They're meant to breathe, move, and change the world. Let your vision come alive - one action, one collaboration, one bold step at a time. You're not scattered. You're expansive. Let's channel your brilliance into real-world breakthroughs.

The Visionary

Welcome to the realm of big dreams, future horizons, and ideas so dazzling they practically need sunglasses. The Visionary sees what others don't - even when no one else is ready. You're driven by the thrill of possibility and the belief that imagination *is* the blueprint for innovation.

You walk the same path as **Walt Disney**, who imagined entire worlds of magic before anyone believed they could be built. Or **Jeff Bezos**, who took a modest online bookstore and turned it into a force that redefined how the world shops, ships, and shares. Visionaries stretch the limits. They live in "what could be," long before it becomes what is.

But even vision needs translation. When your gaze is always 10 steps ahead, it's easy to lose your footing in the now. Your challenge - and your brilliance - is finding the right bridges between dreaming and doing.

How to Spot a Visionary

- Starts sentences with, "What if we…" more often than not.
- Thinks five years ahead (and forgets today's deadline).
- Bristles at phrases like "that's just how it's done."
- Feels bored with small talk - wants to talk big picture, big impact.
- Gets lit up by a whiteboard and a willing audience.
- Team frequently says, "Whoa… that's ambitious" (and they're not wrong).

Strengths

- Sees opportunities where others see limits.
- Inspires teams with bold, energizing visions.
- Challenges outdated systems with purpose-driven imagination.
- Connects ideas across industries and disciplines.
- Anchors others in *why* the work matters.

Shadow Side

- Can overlook logistics while chasing the next big idea.
- Easily bored once the initial inspiration fades.
- Risks exhausting their team with too many pivots.
- May struggle to simplify their message for others to follow.
- Sometimes gets caught in vision mode without moving to execution.

Emotional Cost (Internal)

When out of sync, Visionaries often feel:

- Emotionally deflated when others can't yet grasp their big-picture thinking
- Alone in their mission, like they always have to be the trailblazer
- Tempted to scrap ideas too early when momentum doesn't match excitement
- Anxious from holding the whole vision alone without help in execution
- Doubtful if the world is really ready for what they're here to bring

Remember: You don't have to carry the future alone. Your vision deserves both belief and support. Let others catch up - it doesn't mean you have to slow down.

Stress Triggers (External)

- "That's not realistic" feedback that stifles innovation
- Environments resistant to change or disruption
- Being left out of planning decisions despite being the visionary
- Pressure to explain the vision before others are ready to listen
- Team cultures that don't leave room for dreaming, only doing

Growth Tips (When to Ask for Help)

- "Who can help me bring this to life without dimming the vision?"
- "What small step would move this from idea to action today?"
- "Am I asking my team to leap… without giving them a landing?"
- "Have I clarified *why* this matters before explaining *how*?"
- "Which vision is truly mine to lead right now?"

Remember: Vision doesn't need to come with a cape. Asking for support *is* leadership.

Least Compatible (But Also Most Growth-Expanding)

Say hello to your favorite frenemy: The Organizer.

You're dreaming of galaxies. They're making spreadsheets. While you're focused on transformation, they're focused on timelines.

You might see them as rigid or overly obsessed with the details.
They might see you as chaotic, scattered, or forever moving the goalpost.

The truth? You need each other.

Your vision provides meaning. Their structure provides movement. A brilliant idea doesn't just need wings - it needs a runway.

So, when the tension rises, breathe through it and try this mantra:

"Details give wings to big dreams.
And big dreams give purpose to details."

Dream Team Suggestions

Your vision deserves to breathe, expand, and *happen*. Here's your all-star team:

- **The Strategist** – Aligns your big idea with a long-term plan and sustainable model.
- **The Executor** – Gets boots on the ground to turn ideas into daily action.
- **The Analyst** – Tests your concept with data so it doesn't just *sound* good - it *works*.
- **The Implementer** – Keeps systems flowing and projects on track as you look ahead.
- **The Mentor** – Holds your highest potential while helping you pace the journey.

Bottom Line: You light the path - this team helps you walk it. With structure, data, momentum, and soul-aligned guidance behind you, your vision doesn't just stay big - it becomes real, sustainable, and wildly impactful.

Business Wisdom for the Visionary

You were born to lead with imagination. But don't forget: a dream with no delivery plan is just a wish.

Here is your brilliance-in-action alignment guide:

- Prioritize your visions. Not everything needs to happen at once.
- Find partners who love details and logistics as much as you love the big picture.
- Simplify your message so others can rally around your "why."
- Ground your passion with pacing - burnout is not a badge of honor.
- Celebrate traction, not just transformation.

☑ Own your role as a Visionary. The future needs your imagination.

☑ Don't fear structure - embrace the partners who thrive in it.

☑ Keep painting bold pictures - and trust your team to fill in the strokes.

Your gift is not just seeing what's possible - it's helping the rest of us believe it's possible, too.

A note to you: Visionary, you are *possibility* in human form. You don't just dream of a better future - you *see* it, feel it, speak it into being. Your imagination expands what's possible for everyone around you. But remember this: your ideas are powerful *because of you*, not in spite of you. You don't have to carry the whole vision alone. Let others support the building while you keep your eyes on the horizon. You're not "too much."

You're just early. And the world is catching up. Let's give your dreams the wings - and the roots - they deserve.

Structure & Implementation Energy

"Where smart systems turn big ideas into real results."

Welcome, Architect.

If this Energy of Brilliance™ feels like home, it's because you know something that others often miss - big dreams don't mean much if they never make it past the sticky note stage.

You're not just about doing the work - you're about doing it *well*. You're the one in the room who asks, "Great idea… what's the plan?" And while the world chases shiny objects, *you* quietly make sure the wheels don't fall off.

This Energy is where structure becomes strategy.
Where timelines meet transformation.
Where people trust you - not just because you care, but because you *deliver*.

Why This Energy of Brilliance™ Matters

People in this Energy are often the steady hands behind bold moves. You're the reason things get launched, delivered, and done *well*. You're the process whisperer. The list-maker. The dot-connector. You notice the details that others miss - and you fix what's broken before most people even know something's wrong.

Your brilliance shows up in:

- Profit stability - because you track, manage, and anticipate
- Operational ease - because you make smart systems feel seamless
- Less burnout - because you distribute the weight, not just carry it
- Room to grow - because you build the kind of foundation that scales

But let's name the hard stuff, too.

You might:

- Feel buried under the weight of too many moving pieces
- Wonder if you're "the only one" holding it all together
- Feel like the dreamers get the spotlight... while you keep the lights on

Here's the truth:

You are not the assistant to the vision - you're the *engine* of it.

Your structure is sacred.

Your way of thinking is what allows the brilliance of others to thrive without collapsing.

You're not boring.

You're essential.

How This Energy Might Show Up for You

If this is your Energy, you may:

- Feel energized by creating order out of chaos
- Have a love-hate relationship with project management tools

- Get lit up by checklists, workflows, and time-saving templates
- Feel anxious when others "wing it" with no plan
- Take deep satisfaction in knowing things are running *smoothly*

You don't just make things happen.

You make them happen *on time, with systems and repeatable success.*

Your Brilliance in Action

At your best, you:

- Break down big visions into doable action steps
- Build out systems that *actually work* for real people
- Keep projects (and people) on track
- Make scaling feel *possible*, not overwhelming
- Give others the confidence to trust the process - because *you've got this*

You are a permission slip to rest.

You're the *reason* others feel safe enough to dream.

What Fuels You

You're at your best when you have:

- A clear plan and defined expectations
- Efficient tools or systems that actually save time
- Time to organize, prioritize, and build out workflows
- A team or partner who follows through
- The freedom to *optimize*, not just execute

What Might Drain You

- Vague tasks with unclear roles
- People changing the plan at the last minute (*without telling you*)
- Feeling like the "default manager" for everyone's chaos
- Micromanagement or having your systems questioned
- Burnout from carrying too much of the execution weight alone

You're not overwhelmed because you're weak.

You're overwhelmed because people keep tossing "just one more thing" on top of your genius.

Your Strengths

- Creating order, flow, and structure
- Turning ideas into action
- Seeing the small details *and* the big picture
- Spotting inefficiencies and fixing them fast
- Designing systems that support others

Your Growth Opportunities

- Saying yes to too much because "you're good at it"
- Staying in planning mode too long before taking action
- Feeling like you have to do it all yourself
- Downplaying your creativity because it doesn't look "artsy"
- Resisting change when you've already built the system

Reminder:

Structure is creative.

You're not just organizing - you're **engineering possibilities.**

Tips for Thriving in This Energy

- **Block time for deep work.** You thrive when you can get into flow without distractions.
- **Build systems that serve *you*,** not just your clients. You deserve ease, too.
- **Document and delegate.** If you've created it once, it doesn't need to live in your head forever.
- **Celebrate completion.** You're always onto the next thing - don't skip your own wins.
- **Know your limits.** Your brilliance deserves to be supported, not stretched thin.

Business Tips for the Builder Brain

- Invest in tools that bring calm and clarity - your tech stack should work *with* you.
- Package your process - clients will pay for your efficiency if you show the value.
- Say no to chaos clients. If they don't respect structure, they don't respect your Energy.
- Collaborate with Visionaries who need your brilliance to ground their ideas.

- Build in *real rest*. You can't run systems at 100% without rebooting, too.

Remember: your gift isn't just building frameworks - it's making success sustainable for everyone involved.

Ready to Go Deeper?

You've uncovered your Structure & Implementation Energy. Now it's time to get even more specific.

Turn the page to take the quiz and discover your **archetype** - the unique way your brilliance shows up in your workflow, leadership style, and business rhythm.

Let's find out how *you* build best.

Discover Your Archetype Quiz

Instructions: For each question, choose the answer that feels most true for you. Go with your first instinct - you can always reflect more deeply afterward!

1. When you start a new project, your first instinct is to:

A) Create a step-by-step plan, timelines, and checklists to keep everything organized.

B) Identify the key actions and jump in to get things moving fast.

C) Figure out practical details and hands-on steps to make sure things will actually work.

2. People often praise you for:

A) Your ability to keep things orderly and structured.

B) How quickly you get things done and make decisions.

C) Your knack for working out the practical, real-life execution of plans.

3. When facing tight deadlines, you:

A) Make sure every task is accounted for and scheduled.

B) Take charge and push the team to meet the goal.

C) Roll up your sleeves and focus on solving immediate problems.

4. Routine and established systems feel:

A) Comforting - they help you stay in control and avoid chaos.

B) Useful, as long as they don't slow things down.

C) Necessary to keep operations running smoothly, though sometimes you'll tweak them to improve efficiency.

5. Your biggest frustration at work is:

A) Disorganization and things being left to chance.

B) People dragging their feet or hesitating to act.

C) Plans that look good on paper but fall apart in real life.

6. When collaborating with others, you:

A) Love to clarify everyone's roles and create structure.

B) Prefer to lead the charge and keep everyone focused on action.

C) Enjoy being the person who figures out how to *actually* implement the plan.

---

7. Your ideal workday includes:

A) Organizing systems, managing schedules, and keeping things in order.

B) Checking off major tasks and seeing fast progress.

C) Solving real-world problems and ensuring plans run smoothly.

---

8. You feel most fulfilled when:

A) Everything is organized and running efficiently.

B) You've driven a project across the finish line.

C) You've turned plans into practical, working reality.

---

9. Under stress, you're more likely to:

A) Double down on organizing to regain control.

B) Push even harder to keep things moving.

C) Focus on troubleshooting immediate issues to keep things working.

---

10. In your mind, true success means:

A) Creating systems that keep business running like a well-oiled machine.

B) Achieving results quickly and decisively.

C) Seeing ideas successfully translated into real-world outcomes.

Scoring

- Mostly A's → You're The Organizer.
- Mostly B's → You're The Executor.
- Mostly C's → You're The Implementer.

Archetypes in This Energy of Brilliance™

The Organizer

Welcome to the world of color-coded calendars, perfectly labeled folders, and a deep love for a solid plan. The Organizer is methodical, precise, and wired to transform chaos into calm. You're the human equivalent of an Excel pivot table - and proud of it.

You're the person teams rely on to make sure nothing falls through the cracks, no matter how many spinning plates are in the air. But your devotion to structure can sometimes leave little room for spontaneity - or the occasional messy brilliance of a last-minute idea.

Think of people like **Marie Kondo**, who turned tidying into a global phenomenon because clutter simply did not spark joy, or **Tim Cook**, who took Apple's vision and ensured it ran like clockwork with quiet discipline and operational excellence. Organizers look at the world and think, *"This could run so much smoother - and I know exactly how."*

How to Spot an Organizer

- Starts sentences with "Let's get organized…"
- Owns more highlighters than most office supply stores stock.
- Feels physically itchy when someone says, "Let's just wing it."
- Has a spreadsheet… for their spreadsheets.
- Calmly untangles chaos while everyone else is panicking.
- Is the reason the team knows what's happening, when, and how.

Strengths

- Creates clear plans, schedules, and systems.
- Keeps teams and projects moving smoothly.
- Calm under pressure - even when chaos reigns.
- Meticulous about details and follow-through.
- Anticipates problems before they arise.

Shadow Side

- Can become rigid or resistant to sudden changes.
- May come off as controlling or overly strict.
- Struggles with ambiguity or fast-moving pivots.
- Risks stifling creativity by clinging to systems.

Emotional Cost (Internal)

Being the backbone is no joke. When you're stretched thin, you might feel:

- Anxiety from the pressure to keep every plate spinning
- Frustrated when carefully built plans are ignored or derailed
- Unseen and feeling like your behind-the-scenes brilliance is taken for granted
- Tense when forced to improvise without prep time
- Trapped in the belief that if you don't handle it, no one will

Remember: When this happens, you might retreat into reworking timelines, fixing spreadsheets, or clinging to your calendar for control. That's not avoidance - it's your nervous system seeking stability.

Stress Triggers (External)

- Last-minute changes with no time to recalibrate
- Vague directions or unclear expectations
- Teammates who resist or disregard structure
- Compressed timelines that ignore planning realities
- Environments that celebrate spontaneity over systems

Growth Tips (When to Ask for Help)

When your inner Organizer is tying itself in knots, ask yourself:

- Where could a little flexibility actually make things easier?
- Who on my team thrives on uncertainty - and how can I lean on them?
- Am I clinging to a process because it's truly necessary, or just because it's familiar?
- Could this project survive being "good enough" instead of perfect?
- How might creative input improve my systems, rather than disrupt them?

Remember: your systems are brilliant - but sometimes brilliance also needs a little room to breathe.

Least Compatible (But Also Most Growth-Expanding)

Say hello to your favorite frenemy: The Visionary.

You're the structure. They're the spontaneity. While you're setting milestones and timelines, they're sketching castles in the clouds.

You might see them as chaotic, unrealistic, or constantly moving the goalposts.

They might see you as rigid, inflexible, or resistant to big change.

The truth? You need each other.

Their bold dreams get grounded in your step-by-step brilliance. Your systems make sure those dreams don't evaporate.

Take a breath and try this mantra:

"Details give wings to big dreams - and big dreams give purpose to details."

Dream Team Suggestions

Even the best Organizer shouldn't carry the weight alone. Your systems shine brightest when supported by the right team:

- **The Communicator** – Bridges gaps and keeps everyone informed, so your plans don't live only in your head.
- **The Executor** – Turns your plans into action with precision and speed.
- **The Analyst** – Adds data-driven insights to refine your systems.
- **The Implementer** – Helps maintain your processes in day-to-day operations.
- **The Peacemaker** – Smooths out tension when structure feels constraining to creative teammates.

Bottom line: Together, your dream team helps transform your organizational genius into sustainable, collective success.

Business Wisdom for the Organizer

You don't just manage details - you make momentum possible.

Your magic lies in making things work smoothly so others can shine. But don't forget - *you* shine too.

Here's your brilliance-in-action alignment guide:

- Let flexibility be part of your formula - not a flaw in it.
- Celebrate progress as much as perfect plans.
- Build systems that support people, not just processes.
- Partner with big-picture thinkers to keep your methods fresh and forward-facing.
- Make rest a non-negotiable - your mind runs best when it's not overloaded.

Own your role as an Organizer. You are the grounding wire in any powerful idea.

Don't mistake control for clarity - sometimes the best systems are co-created.

Let go of the pressure to be flawless. The magic is in consistency, not perfection.

Your gift is turning chaos into calm, ideas into action, and overwhelm into order. Without you, innovation would fizzle, and plans would stall. You don't just support the mission - you *sustain* it.

A note to you: Organizer, you are the anchor in the storm, the quiet brilliance behind the scenes. You don't need the spotlight to make a difference - but don't shrink, either. Your contribution isn't just valuable - it's vital. You weren't meant to do it all. You were meant to build what matters. Trust yourself. Trust your systems. And trust that letting go sometimes creates space for your next-level brilliance.

The Executor

Welcome to the realm of checklists, timelines, and the quiet satisfaction of crossing things off the to-do list. The Executor is practical, reliable, and fiercely dedicated to making things happen. You're the person who turns ideas into reality - the engine that keeps businesses moving forward.

You're energized by progress and take genuine pride in delivering results. But sometimes, your strong focus on execution can leave little space for big-picture brainstorming or unexpected changes that might, in truth, make things even better.

Think of people like **Sheryl Sandberg**, who helped transform Facebook from a scrappy startup into a structured global giant through relentless focus on systems and results. Or **Howard Schultz**, who didn't just dream about coffee culture but meticulously built Starbucks into a worldwide brand by ensuring operational excellence at every level.

Executors are the steady hands who make sure visions don't stay stuck on a whiteboard. Your practical mind ensures businesses not only survive - but thrive.

How to Spot an Executor

- Thinks "what's the next step?" even while finishing the current one
- Loves a good checklist - possibly color-coded

- Finds satisfaction in meeting deadlines (and sometimes setting them earlier)
- Gently side-eyes people who keep changing their minds
- Feels deeply unsettled by "winging it"
- Team often says, "We'd be lost without them"

Strengths

- Highly dependable and results-driven
- Excellent at following through on plans
- Strong time and task management skills
- Keeps teams focused and moving forward
- Practical and realistic decision-making

Shadow Side

- Can resist new or unconventional ideas
- May become rigid when plans change unexpectedly
- Tends to micromanage details if trust isn't established
- Sometimes struggles to connect daily tasks to the bigger vision
- Risks burning out by carrying too much responsibility

Emotional Cost (Internal)

Carrying the responsibility for follow-through can wear you down. When energy dips, you might feel:

- Resentful when you're doing the heavy lifting alone
- Overwhelmed by unclear priorities or shifting plans
- Isolated from being so deep in the "doing" that connection fades

- Irritated when others can't seem to make a decision
- Drained from always being the dependable one

Remember: These moments might nudge you into solo mode, gravitate you toward structured tasks, or leave you quietly burnt out. Your reliability is a gift - but it deserves rest, too.

Stress Triggers (External)

- Constantly changing instructions with no clarity
- Teams that can't make or stick to decisions
- Work environments where priorities shift daily
- Overbooking or excessive delegation to "the one who gets it done"
- Being asked to "wing it" without a roadmap

Growth Tips (When to Ask for Help)

When your drive becomes a source of strain rather than strength, reflect on these questions:

- Am I leaving space for creative input from others?
- What small changes could help me be more adaptable?
- Who can I trust to help carry the workload?
- Am I focused on urgent tasks… or truly important ones?
- How often do I connect my daily work to the broader vision?

Remember: you don't have to shoulder it all alone. You're strongest when you balance doing with collaborating.

Least Compatible (But Also Most Growth-Expanding)

Say hello to your favorite frenemy: The Visionary.

You're the master of execution. They're the architect of imagination. While you're triple-checking a deadline, they're rewriting the plan…again.

You may see them as impractical, unrealistic, or allergic to structure. They may see you as rigid, overly cautious, or resistant to their next big idea.

The truth? You both want the same thing: impact.
You build it through consistency. They chase it through innovation.

When you learn to meet in the middle - their dream, your drive - magic happens.
So the next time a Visionary upends your checklist, try this mantra:

> **"Flexibility doesn't mean chaos - it can create new paths to efficiency."**

Dream Team Suggestions

Your drive for results is unstoppable - but it becomes even more powerful when paired with the right partners. Here's your ideal support crew:

- **The Innovator** → Brings creative solutions that keep execution fresh and relevant.
- **The Communicator** → Helps clarify plans and ensures smooth collaboration.
- **The Strategist** → Connects your daily actions to long-term business goals.

- **The Networker** → Expands relationships and opportunities that fuel progress.
- **The Peacemaker** → Maintains harmony when deadlines or intensity rise.

Bottom line: You're the engine - but even engines need great fuel and a strong crew.

Business Wisdom for the Executor

You don't just check boxes - you carry dreams across the finish line. Your gift is in the doing. But doing doesn't mean doing *everything* alone.

Here's your brilliance-in-action alignment guide:

- Welcome fresh ideas, even when they disrupt your flow - they're how progress begins.
- Trust your team - delegation isn't a weakness, it's how you build momentum that lasts.
- Zoom out often to reconnect with the bigger picture - your work fuels something greater.
- Celebrate progress along the way, not just completion - you deserve to feel proud *before* the checklist is done.
- Let adaptability be your ally - when things shift, you don't break... you evolve.

☑ Own your role as an Executor. You are the traction beneath every great idea.

☑ Don't confuse being busy with being aligned - your impact deepens when your "yes" is intentional.

☑ Stay open to flow - but protect your energy from overcommitment. You *are* the backbone, not the entire body.

Your gift is turning vision into tangible progress. Without you, dreams stay on dry erase boards. You make the mission real - day by day, task by task, result by result.

A note to you: Executor, you are the engine behind achievement. The finisher. The force that turns "we should" into "we did." Your reliability is a rare kind of brilliance - one that too often goes uncelebrated. But make no mistake: you are the reason things move forward. Don't just survive the workload - design one that serves *you*, too. You're not here to carry it all. You're here to build what matters. Let your drive be met with support, and your pace be paired with purpose.

The Implementer

Welcome to the world of getting things done - reliably, precisely, and without unnecessary fuss. The Implementer is practical, steady, and the master of translating plans into real-world action. You're the one who ensures that brilliant ideas don't stay trapped on whiteboards but actually make it into the hands of customers or into daily operations.

You thrive on clear instructions, dependable routines, and processes that work. For you, there's comfort in knowing what comes next - and satisfaction in seeing tangible results.

Think of people like **Mary Barra**, who's transforming General Motors by not only envisioning an all-electric future but also putting in place the manufacturing, supply chain, and operational shifts needed to make it real. Or **Indra Nooyi**, who as CEO of PepsiCo didn't just dream up big ideas but meticulously implemented strategies that transformed the business while keeping operations humming. Implementers bring visions down to earth - and make sure they stay there.

But your gift for reliability can sometimes become a double-edged sword. Change can feel disruptive. Unproven ideas might look risky. And collaborating with big-picture dreamers can sometimes leave you wondering, "But how exactly are we supposed to do that?"

Still, the world desperately needs you. Without Implementers, businesses would drown in half-finished projects and brilliant-but-unexecuted plans. You're the stabilizing force that makes success sustainable.

How to Spot an Implementer

- Smiles when handed a checklist - and immediately starts checking things off.
- Loves knowing exactly what's expected and when it's due.
- Looks slightly panicked when someone suggests "let's just wing it."
- Often the first to say, "Great idea... how are we actually going to do this?"
- Keeps teams calm during chaos by sticking to practical steps.
- Has color-coded folders (either physical or digital) - and can actually find things in them.

Strengths

- Highly reliable and steady under pressure.
- Exceptional at turning ideas into actionable, concrete steps.
- Thrives in structured environments with well-defined tasks.
- Ensures consistency and high quality in results.
- Provides stability and predictability that teams can rely on.

Shadow Side

- Resistant to change or experimenting with untested methods.
- May become inflexible or overly rigid when routines are disrupted.

- Sometimes struggles to see the bigger picture beyond immediate tasks.
- Can dismiss creative or unconventional ideas as impractical.

Emotional Cost (Internal)

Your consistency creates flow, but unpredictability can knock you off center. When you're off balance, you might feel:

- Uneasy when routines are disrupted without notice
- Irritated by vague goals or unclear expectations
- Stressed when abstract ideas replace clear steps
- Frustrated when others ignore proven systems
- Emotionally shut down when asked to pivot too fast, too often

Remember: In these moments, you may double down on routines, quietly withdraw, or resist change out of self-protection. That's not stubbornness - it's your brilliance craving structure.

Stress Triggers (External)

- Rapid shifts in direction without clear communication
- Ambiguous project goals or scattered leadership
- Big-idea teams that overlook essential details
- High-speed environments with no room to stabilize
- Pressure to innovate before the basics are nailed down

Growth Tips (When to Ask for Help)

- Embrace occasional change as a chance for improvement rather than a disruption.

- Partner with Visionaries who bring new ideas - they'll help expand your comfort zone without leaving you adrift.
- Work with Strategists to connect your day-to-day tasks to broader goals.
- Allow yourself small experiments within safe parameters to test new approaches.

Remember: adapting doesn't mean abandoning what works. It means strengthening it.

Least Compatible (But Also Most Growth-Expanding)

Say hello to your favorite frenemy: The Innovator.

You're diligently following a proven process, and they burst in declaring, "Let's scrap the whole thing and try something totally new!"

You may see Innovators as disruptive, impractical, or even reckless. They might feel stifled by your steady pace or eyeroll your need for step-by-step plans.

But neither of you is wrong - you're just building success from different starting points.

Together, you can strike a powerful balance between breakthrough ideas and grounded implementation.

Try this mantra:

"Every new idea deserves a fair test - and every test deserves a clear plan."

Dream Team Suggestions

You're unstoppable when surrounded by a team that complements your practical genius. Here's your ideal crew:

- **The Visionary** – Inspires you with big-picture thinking and new ideas you might not have considered.
- **The Analyst** – Brings thorough analysis and risk assessment to ensure your work is effective and sustainable.
- **The Communicator** – Bridges gaps between practical tasks and team understanding, helping everyone stay aligned.
- **The Organizer** – Supports your systems and helps keep projects structured and on track.
- **The Networker** – Connects your practical efforts to external resources and fresh opportunities.

Bottom line: You bring structure to vision - and your team keeps that structure responsive and resilient.

Business Wisdom for the Implementer

You're not just a doer - you're the rhythm that makes progress sustainable. You create flow where others create friction, and that is its own kind of genius.

Here's your brilliance-in-action alignment guide:

- Embrace new ideas with curiosity - not fear. Innovation needs your grounding, not your resistance.

- Let your routines support you - but don't let them become cages. Flexibility doesn't cancel out consistency.
- Balance reliability with creativity - you're at your best when structure and imagination coexist.
- Communicate your needs clearly - you deserve to work in systems that respect your pace.
- Ask for clarity when direction feels fuzzy - you bring things to life, and that requires a clear blueprint.

☑ Own your role as an Implementer. You are the steady hand that brings order to vision.

☑ Don't underestimate the power of repetition - it's what builds trust, mastery, and legacy.

☑ Let your voice be heard - not just in the doing, but in the planning. You deserve a seat at the strategy table.

Your gift is showing the world what reliable brilliance looks like. You bring structure to possibility - and without you, execution would stall before it starts.

A note to you: Implementer, you are the pulse of progress. The one who keeps the wheels turning when the world gets distracted by shiny ideas. You may not always be the loudest voice in the room - but you are the one who makes sure things *actually happen*. Remember, your steadiness is a superpower. But don't let it silence your insight. You're not just here to carry out plans - you're here to help shape them. So, take up space. Raise your hand. Share what you see. Because your brilliance isn't just in doing the work - it's in knowing *exactly* what makes the work *work*.

Strategy & Foresight Energy

"Where clarity becomes your compass - and wisdom becomes your superpower."

If you've landed here, you're not the type to act just to *look* busy. You move with intention. You question. You analyze. You plan.
And while some rush to act, you pause to *think*. Not because you're afraid - but because you care enough to get it right.

This is the Energy of Brilliance™ where thoughtfulness isn't a delay - it's your edge. You're the one who brings calm to chaos, structure to vision, and a long game to every wild idea.

I see you. Because this Energy has been my anchor more times than I can count.
When systems were breaking down and everything felt unpredictable, it wasn't charm that carried me through - it was this:

- The ability to zoom out, look at the full picture, and ask better questions.
- The instinct to pause and *build a plan*, not just a quick fix.
- The clarity to know when to act - and the courage to wait when the time wasn't right.

Why This Energy of Brilliance™ Matters

Let's be honest: in a world that rewards hustle and flashy moves, slow thinkers often get overlooked. But here's what most people forget - *strategy is speed made sustainable.*

This Energy brings the kind of brilliance that might not be loud, but it's lasting.

You:

- Spot patterns long before they become problems
- Ask questions no one else thinks to ask
- Build systems and solutions that outlive trends
- Help others feel grounded, informed, and prepared

And yes, it can be heavy sometimes.

You might:

- Struggle with analysis paralysis
- Feel invisible because your wins happen behind the scenes
- Carry the pressure of needing to "get it right" for everyone
- Watch people act impulsively while you're still connecting the dots

But let me say this clearly:

- Your pause is not weakness - it's wisdom.
- Your vision isn't slow - it's strategic.
- Your mind doesn't wander - it *leads*.

How This Energy Might Show Up for You

If this is your Energy, you may:

- Think 10 steps ahead - sometimes without realizing it
- Feel most alive when you're solving a complex puzzle
- Get frustrated when decisions are made without data or logic
- Thrive in roles where your insight can guide others
- Find calm in planning - and chaos in uncertainty

You're the quiet visionary, the analyst, the strategist, the specialist.

Whatever form it takes, your Energy isn't reaction - it's precision.

Your Brilliance in Action

At your best, you:

- Turn confusion into clarity
- Craft sustainable strategies, not quick wins
- Bring depth to conversations and depth to leadership
- Prevent disasters before anyone else sees them coming
- Offer advice and insight that people return to *years* later

You don't chase the spotlight.

You build the roadmap.

And that's where real power lies.

What Fuels You

You're at your best when you have:

- Space to think before acting

- Data to support your decisions
- Trusted people to bounce big ideas off of
- Clear goals with long-term vision
- Time to go deep into your craft or expertise

What Might Drain You

- Vague or rushed expectations
- Environments that value speed over sustainability
- Feeling responsible for "figuring it all out" alone
- Watching your ideas be ignored - only to be needed later
- Burnout from carrying the emotional load of *always being prepared*

You don't need to be "faster."

You need support that honors your pace and process.

Your Strengths

- Strategic clarity and long-term vision
- Solving complex problems with elegance
- Turning information into insight
- Helping others feel prepared and calm
- Thinking before acting - and acting with purpose

Your Growth Opportunities

- Getting stuck in the planning stage
- Worrying you'll never know *enough* to begin
- Hesitating to delegate because no one "does it right"
- Feeling like your gifts aren't "exciting" enough

- Doubting your brilliance because it's not always visible

Reminder:

You are the blueprint.

You are the reason things last.

Tips for Thriving in This Energy

- Create time blocks for planning *and* implementation - progress doesn't require perfection
- Collaborate with action-oriented partners who can help move your ideas forward
- Celebrate the clarity you bring - even if others don't notice it at first
- Trust your instincts - yes, even the intuitive ones
- Let yourself start, even when you don't have every answer

Business Tips for the Strategic Soul

- Document your frameworks and thought processes - this is intellectual property gold
- Package your insight into offers, guides, or systems others can benefit from
- Don't water down your brilliance - find clients who *want* the depth you bring
- Use automation and delegation to free up space for strategy
- Show your value by connecting the dots others miss

Remember: your gift isn't just seeing the path ahead - it's mapping it clearly enough for others to follow with confidence.

Ready to Go Deeper?

You've uncovered your Strategy & Foresight Energy. Now let's explore the unique way your brilliance shows up in your daily workflow, your problem-solving style, and your leadership approach.

Turn the page to take the "Discover Your Archetype" quiz - and learn how your brilliant mind can become your greatest asset for sustainable success.

You don't just plan for the future.

You *design it.*

Discover Your Archetype Quiz

Instructions: Choose the answer that feels most true for you. Trust your instincts - the first thought is often the right one!

1. When faced with a problem, your first instinct is to:

A) Gather all the facts and examine the details thoroughly.

B) Consider how this problem fits into the bigger picture and future plans.

C) Look at it through the lens of your unique area of expertise.

2. People often come to you for:

A) Insightful analysis and spotting hidden details.

B) Strategic guidance and clear plans.

C) Deep, specialized knowledge in a particular field.

3. When tackling a big project, you:

A) Research and analyze every angle to avoid surprises.

B) Create a step-by-step plan that aligns with broader goals.

C) Focus on your specialized contribution, ensuring it's excellent.

4. Routine and structure feel:

A) Essential - it keeps mistakes at bay.

B) Important, but only if it supports long-term goals.

C) Comforting within your specialty, though you prefer mastery over routine tasks.

5. Your biggest frustration at work is:

A) Missing details or sloppy work that creates errors.

B) People acting without considering long-term impacts.

C) Being expected to cover areas outside your specialty.

6. In team settings, you're known for:

A) Digging into the data to uncover important insights.

B) Helping everyone see how their roles fit into the bigger strategy.

C) Bringing expert-level skills that elevate the project's quality.

7. Your perfect workday would include:

A) Solving complex problems and analyzing information.

B) Mapping out a clear strategy and guiding decisions.

C) Diving deep into your specialized area and refining your craft.

---

8. You feel most satisfied when:

A) You've found critical insights others missed.

B) Your plan is executed successfully and moves things forward.

C) You've mastered a new skill or solved a challenging issue in your field.

---

9. Under stress, you're more likely to:

A) Get stuck overanalyzing details.

B) Worry about how decisions affect the bigger picture.

C) Retreat into your area of expertise and avoid unrelated tasks.

---

10. In your mind, success means:

A) Understanding things fully and avoiding errors.

B) Achieving long-term goals through clear planning.

C) Being the go-to expert in your chosen field.

Scoring

- Mostly A's → You're The Analyst.
- Mostly B's → You're The Strategist.
- Mostly C's → You're The Specialist.

Archetypes in This Energy of Brilliance™

The Analyst

Welcome to the domain of deep dives, sharp insights, and the satisfying click of puzzle pieces falling into place. The Analyst is meticulous, insightful, and driven by logic and precision. You bring clarity to chaos, spotting risks and hidden opportunities long before anyone else.

You're the person who reads the fine print, double-checks the numbers, and thinks three steps ahead so the team doesn't fall into avoidable traps. But your dedication to getting it exactly right can sometimes leave you stuck in a loop of endless analysis - or feeling like others are rushing forward without thinking.

Think of people like **Bill Gates**, who turned an obsession with code and logical systems into an empire that redefined modern computing. Or **Mark Zuckerberg**, whose analytical mind and algorithmic thinking helped build a social media machine that thrives on precision, pattern recognition, and calculated growth. Analysts are the ones who ask, "Is this truly the best way?" - and then find the answer.

How to Spot an Analyst

- Asks "Why?" … and then "How?" … and then "What's the data say?"
- Keeps color-coded spreadsheets for everything - even their hobbies.

- Pauses thoughtfully before speaking, even in casual conversations.
- Gets a little twitchy if someone makes a decision based on "gut feeling" alone.
- Team says, "Wow, I never thought of it that way," after hearing their analysis.
- Secretly enjoys reading research reports - for fun.

Strengths

- Exceptionally skilled at critical thinking and problem-solving.
- Excellent attention to detail and accuracy.
- Turns complex data into clear, actionable insights.
- Helps businesses avoid costly mistakes through thorough evaluation.
- Maintains objectivity even under pressure.

Shadow Side

- Can become indecisive when data feels incomplete.
- Tends to overanalyze, delaying decisions or progress.
- May struggle to communicate insights in simple terms.
- Risks getting bogged down in details, losing sight of the big picture.
- Can come across as detached or overly critical.

Emotional Cost (Internal)

Your brain is a high-powered engine - but it can overheat without a cooldown plan. When overloaded, you might feel:

- Mentally drained from overanalyzing every angle

- Anxious when expected to act without enough information
- Frustrated when others skip the details or misinterpret the data
- Dismissed when your insights are overlooked or undervalued
- Disconnected from teams that prize speed over substance

Remember: You might spiral into research rabbit holes or second-guess decisions you've already made. That's not indecision - it's your brilliance craving clarity before commitment.

Stress Triggers (External)

- Pressure to act without data or preparation
- Disorganized teams or vague expectations
- Fast-paced environments that lack structure
- Being shut down when raising red flags
- Colleagues who operate with "gut instinct" over insight

Growth Tips (When to Ask for Help)

When you feel stuck in analysis - or like you're the only one worried about the details - ask yourself:

- Which decision truly needs more data… and which one just needs courage?
- Who can help me simplify my message, so others understand my insights?
- Where might a faster, imperfect action be better than waiting for certainty?
- Am I looking for answers - or avoiding the risk of making a choice?

- Who can balance my caution with momentum?

Remember: Your gift is clarity. But progress sometimes means stepping forward even when the entire puzzle isn't solved.

Least Compatible (But Also Most Growth-Expanding)

Say hello to your favorite frenemy: The Catalyst.

You're carefully examining a spreadsheet, hunting for patterns… and the Catalyst barrels in saying, "Let's just do it!"

You may see Catalysts as reckless or dismissive of risks.
They may view you as slow or resistant to change.

Neither of you is wrong - you just move at different speeds. When paired with mutual respect, you can create brilliant momentum grounded in wisdom.

Try this mantra:

> **"Fast isn't always progress. But slow isn't always safe."**

Dream Team Suggestions

Your insights deserve to see the light of day - and they thrive with the right partners. Here's your ideal crew:

- **The Visionary** → Helps expand your focus beyond the immediate data, connecting your insights to long-term goals.
- **The Communicator** → Translates your detailed findings into language the whole team understands and rallies behind.

- **The Mentor** → Provides perspective, reminding you when it's time to stop analyzing and start acting.
- **The Implementer** → Turns your analysis into real-world actions, ensuring your plans don't stay theoretical.
- **The Networker** → Connects your brilliance to external opportunities, expanding your influence beyond the team.

Bottom line: Together, this team ensures your depth and thoroughness become the foundation for smart, sustainable growth. You provide the clarity. They help turn it into momentum.

Business Wisdom for the Analyst

You are the lens that brings clarity to complexity. While others guess, you guide. While others rush, you refine.

Here's your brilliance-in-action alignment guide:

- Perfect information rarely exists - don't let the search for it become your cage.
- Share your insights simply and clearly - your wisdom only creates change when others can apply it.
- Trust that thoughtful action doesn't have to be reckless - momentum and precision can coexist.
- Give yourself permission to move before the data feels airtight - progress is often the proof, not the prerequisite.
- Balance your gift for analysis with collaboration - others may not see what you see, but that doesn't mean they don't bring value.

☑ Own your role as an Analyst. You elevate conversations with depth and clarity.

☑ Don't fear being misunderstood - practice showing your thought process in a way others can follow.

☑ Remember, your insight is only one part of a thriving team - it doesn't need to be perfect to be powerful.

Your gift is discernment. You don't just see trends - you reveal truths. You make decisions smarter, businesses stronger, and outcomes more aligned with reality.

A note to you: Analyst, your brilliance is quiet - but never small. You see the patterns, the pitfalls, the potential. You don't just ask questions - you ask the *right* ones. But don't get stuck waiting for certainty. Sometimes, the most impactful growth happens in the space between clarity and courage. You're not here to slow the team down - you're here to *sharpen the path forward*. So, keep questioning. Keep refining. But also? Dare to trust your gut. Your brilliance isn't just in what you *know* - it's in how you *move through the unknown.*

The Strategist

Welcome to the realm of long games, big maps, and carefully laid plans. The Strategist is analytical, future-focused, and exceptionally skilled at connecting the dots to create a path forward. You're the one who sees the patterns others miss, weaving together insights into plans that keep businesses moving with purpose and stability.

Your mind naturally zooms out to view the entire chessboard, anticipating moves and consequences. You bring clarity where others see only complexity. But your gift for foresight can sometimes feel like a double-edged sword. People might see you as cautious or reserved, and your deliberate pace may frustrate those hungry for immediate action.

Think of leaders like **Peter Drucker**, the father of modern management, who taught generations to think systematically and strategically. Or **Stephen Covey**, who didn't just help people plan their days - but rethink how their entire lives fit into bigger goals. Strategists like you transform chaos into clear direction and make sure that success isn't just accidental - but sustainable.

How to Spot a Strategist

- Loves frameworks, mind maps, and color-coded spreadsheets.
- Always has a follow-up question: "But what's the goal here?"
- Thinks in timelines - five years out, minimum.

- Can recite strategic models like some people quote song lyrics.
- Gently sighs when people want to "just wing it."
- Team says: "Wow… I never even thought about that angle."

Strengths

- Exceptional at long-term planning and forecasting.
- Skilled at analyzing complex situations and spotting hidden patterns.
- Keeps teams aligned with bigger goals and purpose.
- Calm and objective, even under pressure.
- Thinks ahead to avoid costly pitfalls.

Shadow Side

- May become overly analytical, delaying decisions.
- Can appear emotionally distant or detached.
- Sometimes struggles to act quickly when circumstances demand agility.
- Risks missing immediate opportunities in favor of perfect plans.

Emotional Cost (Internal)

Your gift is foresight, but it can feel like a burden when no one else is looking ahead. When stress creeps in, you might feel:

- Frustrated by short-term thinking and rushed decisions
- Overwhelmed by the mental load of planning for every possibility
- Isolated by your forward focus - like you're solving problems no one sees yet

- Guilty for not acting fast enough, or too fast without certainty
- Exhausted from carrying the responsibility of being the guide

Remember: When you're tapped out, you might slip into silence, rework a plan obsessively, or delay progress in pursuit of perfection. That's not procrastination - it's your care for doing things *right*.

Stress Triggers (External)

- Sudden pivots without strategic backing
- Environments that prize action over alignment
- Being rushed through decisions without time to evaluate risk
- Teams who ignore your insights or question your caution
- Constantly shifting goals that undermine the long game

Growth Tips (When to Ask for Help)

When your strategic mind feels stuck or strained, ask yourself:

- Which decisions truly require more analysis - and which ones need action now?
- How can I communicate my insights, so others feel included, not overwhelmed?
- Who can help me translate my plans into tangible steps?
- Am I so focused on future risks that I'm missing opportunities right in front of me?
- What's one imperfect action I can take today to move things forward?

Remember: The perfect plan means little if it never leaves the page. Your gift is wisdom   and wisdom shines brightest when it's shared in motion.

Least Compatible (But Also Most Growth-Expanding)

Say hello to your favorite frenemy: The Catalyst.

You're carefully mapping out the next five years… and the Catalyst bursts in ready to launch something new tomorrow.

You may see Catalysts as impulsive or dismissive of the risks. They may see you as slow-moving or resistant to progress.

Neither of you is wrong - you just operate on very different tempos. But when paired with trust and mutual respect, you can build brilliant momentum grounded in foresight.

Try this mantra:

"Speed lights the spark. Strategy fuels the fire."

Dream Team Suggestions

Your brilliance shines the brightest when you're surrounded by people who help bring your insights to life. Here's your dream crew:

- **The Executor** → Brings your carefully crafted plans into action, step by step.
- **The Innovator** → Adds fresh, creative solutions that challenge your assumptions.
- **The Communicator** → Makes your complex strategies accessible and engaging for the whole team.

- **The Implementer** → Handles the day-to-day details that transform plans into sustainable systems.
- **The Specialist** → Brings deep expertise that sharpens your strategies and fills knowledge gaps.

Bottom line: Together, this team helps ensure your strategic brilliance isn't just theoretical - it becomes impactful and lasting. You draw the map. They help navigate the journey.

Business Wisdom for the Strategist

You don't just see the big picture - you map the road to get there. While others chase ideas, you chart direction. You turn intention into intelligent action.

Here's your brilliance-in-action alignment guide:

- Your ability to think ahead is rare - own it. Strategy *is* a form of leadership.
- Don't wait for perfect clarity - start with what you *do* know and refine along the way.
- Share your strategy early and often - alignment only happens when your team understands the "why."
- Be willing to adjust the plan without abandoning the vision.
- Trust that your insight has value - even if it's quiet or countercultural.

☑ Own your role as the Strategist. You are the compass in the chaos.

☑ Don't second-guess your slow pace - deliberation is your power, not a flaw.

☑ Let others contribute energy and execution, while you hold the long view with grace.

Your gift is foresight. You anticipate what's around the corner and help others prepare, pivot, and stay grounded through it all.

A note to you: Strategist, you are the stillness in the storm. The one who can see how today's choices shape tomorrow's reality. But don't let your plan become a prison. Strategy is only as strong as your willingness to adapt. You're not here to rush or react - you're here to lead with wisdom, patience, and purposeful direction. Let your guidance shine. Not as control - but as confidence. You're not behind... You're building brilliance that lasts.

The Specialist

Welcome to the world of depth, mastery, and laser-focused excellence. The Specialist is the person whose knowledge runs deeper than most people's curiosity even goes. You're the one who knows the details others gloss over, who can spot a flaw in a process, a pattern in data, or a missing piece in a complex puzzle.

Your mind is a finely tuned instrument in your chosen field. You bring certainty, clarity, and high standards to every project you touch. But your dedication to your niche can sometimes make you feel like you're working on an island, disconnected from the rest of the team - or frustrated when others don't grasp the level of precision you hold dear.

Think of people like **Steve Wozniak**, the brilliant engineer who quietly built the technology that launched Apple and revolutionized personal computing. Or **Serena Williams**, whose unmatched commitment to mastering her craft elevated her to global icon status. Specialists don't just know things - they embody them with precision, passion, and quiet power.

How to Spot a Specialist

- Can talk for hours about one topic - and loves it when someone actually listens.
- Notices tiny details everyone else misses.
- Feels a jolt of joy at the words "deep dive."

- Gets slightly irked when people say, "Let's not get into the weeds."
- Hates being rushed through explanations.
- Becomes the team's "go-to" person for anything in their domain.

Strengths

- Possesses deep expertise and technical excellence in a specific area.
- Delivers exceptionally high-quality, precise work.
- Is the dependable anchor for complex, specialized tasks.
- Constantly pursues learning and mastery.
- Brings credibility, authority, and confidence to projects.

Shadow Side

- Hesitant to step outside their specialty.
- Can become isolated from broader team discussions.
- Sometimes struggles to connect the dots to the bigger business picture.
- Risks undervaluing contributions outside their expertise.
- May appear rigid when others want to "wing it."

Emotional Cost (Internal)

Your mastery is your magic - but being the go-to can take a toll. When out of balance, you might feel:

- Frustrated when people oversimplify your area of expertise
- Resentful when asked to step outside your zone without support
- Misunderstood or isolated because few grasp your depth
- Unseen when your precision is taken for granted

- Defensive when your well-informed advice is brushed off

Remember: In these moments, you might bury yourself in solo work or retreat to your niche. That's not stubbornness - it's you seeking a space where your genius is fully respected.

Stress Triggers (External)

- Pressure to multitask or wear too many hats
- Environments that prioritize speed over quality
- Colleagues who devalue depth or skip the "why"
- Being expected to simplify complex ideas with no time
- Being dismissed as "too detailed" when clarity is needed most

Growth Tips (When to Ask for Help)

When your specialized brilliance starts feeling like a cage instead of a superpower, ask yourself:

- How can I share my expertise in ways others can easily grasp?
- Who can help me connect my work to the team's bigger goals?
- Where might collaboration bring in fresh ideas into my niche?
- Am I isolating myself instead of contributing my voice to team discussions?
- How can I stay open to change without compromising my standards?

Remember: your depth is invaluable - but even the deepest well needs to flow outward.

Least Compatible (But Also Most Growth-Expanding)

Say hello to your favorite frenemy: the Peacemaker.

Imagine you're carefully perfecting a system… and the Peacemaker is gently asking you to adjust it because it's "upsetting the group vibe."

The Specialist's unwavering focus on precision can clash with the Peacemaker's desire for team harmony and emotional equilibrium.

You may see Peacemakers as too accommodating or loose with standards. They may view you as inflexible or unwilling to adapt for the sake of unity.

Neither of you is wrong - you just value different things. Together, you can create incredible balance… once you learn to speak each other's language.

If you're working with a Peacemaker, try this mantra:

"Harmony and high standards can coexist - but only through clear communication."

Dream Team Suggestions

Your brilliance deserves a team who can help your depth make the biggest impact. Here's your ideal crew:

- **The Visionary**: Helps you connect your niche expertise to the broader future.
- **The Communicator**: Translates your technical insights for others so they're not lost in jargon.
- **The Organizer**: Creates systems that allow your expertise to shine efficiently.

- **The Catalyst**: Inspires you to apply your skills in innovative, unexpected ways.
- **The Mentor**: Guides you in using your depth to influence and teach others beyond your immediate field.

Bottom line: You bring the precision. They help you build the bridge from mastery to momentum.

Business Wisdom for the Specialist

You don't just know your craft - you embody it. Your mastery raises the bar and deepens the impact of every project you touch.

Here's your brilliance-in-action alignment guide:

- Own your expertise - it's not arrogance, it's alignment.
- Don't hide behind perfection - your value shines even when you're still refining.
- Share what you know - teaching is leadership, and your voice matters.
- Keep learning - your curiosity keeps your brilliance sharp.
- Let others into your process - collaboration doesn't dilute your depth, it expands your reach.

☑ Embrace your role as the Specialist. You bring precision, purpose, and power to the table.

☑ Don't shrink to fit - stand tall in your standards and let your work speak volumes.

☑ Know that mastery isn't final - it's a lifelong evolution, and that's part of the magic.

Your gift is turning complexity into clarity. You don't just do it well - you elevate how well it *can* be done.

A note to you: Specialist, you are the deep well in a world of surface scrolls. The quiet force that makes excellence look effortless. But brilliance isn't meant to hide in the shadows. Your insight deserves a spotlight. You're not just here to perfect your craft - you're here to shape industries, mentor minds, and inspire what's possible. Let your mastery be seen, felt, and shared. The world needs your depth.

Relationships & Communication Energy

"Where connection builds the bridge - and communication carries the spark."

If you've landed here, chances are you've always been the one who just *knows* how people feel.

You read between the lines.

You hear what isn't being said.

You remember birthdays, follow up on hard conversations, and sense when someone's energy is just... off.

This is the Energy of Brilliance™ where connection isn't a "nice to have" - it's the foundation.

And for you, business isn't just about what you offer - it's about *how people feel when they experience it.*

That's your brilliance. That's your gift.

I want you to know: this Energy has been one of my deepest teachers.

I've built entire communities by listening - really listening - to what people *need.*

And I've also burned out by trying to hold space for too many hearts at once.

So, if you've ever thought:

- "Why do I feel so much?"
- "Why does this client relationship affect me more than it should?"

- "Why am I always the one people confide in?"

You're not alone. You're not "too sensitive."

You're powerful.

And this Energy of Brilliance™ is where your power lives.

Why This Energy of Brilliance™ Matters

In a world chasing algorithms and automation, *you* bring the human back into business.

You're the reason clients feel seen - not just sold to.

You're the reason teams feel safe - not just productive.

And you're the reason relationships turn into referrals, collaborations, and community.

You:

- Build trust before transactions
- Remember the details that make people feel valued
- Bridge differences with compassion and clarity
- Infuse warmth into every message, meeting, and milestone

But yes, it can also be heavy.

You might:

- Absorb others' energy and emotions
- Avoid conflict even when boundaries are needed
- Feel responsible for "keeping the peace"

- Struggle to say no, especially when someone needs your help

Let's be real: it's exhausting to always be the glue.

But that doesn't mean your Energy is a burden.

It means it's sacred.

How This Energy Might Show Up for You

If this is your Energy, you may:

- Light up in 1:1 conversations or group settings where real talk flows
- Feel drained after surface-level small talk or emotionally intense interactions
- Be the person others turn to when they need to talk something out
- Love storytelling, writing, or speaking as a way to share truth and connect
- Use your voice to champion others - and sometimes forget to champion yourself

You're the communicator, the connector, the host, the harmonizer.

You don't just *talk*.

You *transmit* understanding.

Your Brilliance in Action

At your best, you:

- Spark meaningful conversations that open minds and hearts
- Build strong, lasting networks rooted in mutual respect

- Translate feelings into action - whether in copy, speech, or leadership
- De-escalate tension with compassion and clarity
- Inspire loyalty by making people feel like they belong

You don't just have emotional intelligence.

You *lead with it*.

And in today's business world? That's your edge.

What Fuels You

You thrive when you have:

- Safe spaces for authentic conversation
- Clients or collaborators who value empathy as much as execution
- Opportunities to use your voice - on stage, in writing, or in deep discussion
- Time to reflect on interpersonal dynamics and how you show up
- A supportive community where *you* feel seen and heard

What Might Drain You

Your Energy wanes when you face:

- Cold, transactional environments
- Constantly holding space for others without being poured into
- People-pleasing patterns that override your boundaries
- Misalignment between what you say and what you feel
- Feedback that dismisses the value of relationships or "soft skills"

Just because you're good at handling emotions doesn't mean you should have to handle *everyone's*.

Your Strengths

- Emotional intelligence and empathy
- Storytelling and clear, heartfelt communication
- Building meaningful relationships and trust
- Resolving conflict with grace
- Making others feel seen, safe, and supported

Your Growth Opportunities

- Overextending yourself emotionally
- Avoiding hard conversations to "keep the peace"
- Doubting your value in numbers-driven environments
- Forgetting to protect your own energy
- Holding on to relationships that no longer serve you

Reminder:

You don't need to fix everything.

You just need to honor your truth.

Tips for Thriving in This Energy

- Create intentional space for your own emotions - not just others'
- Practice saying no without guilt (your "yes" is sacred)
- Use systems to support your communication so you're not always "on"

- Celebrate how your words make people feel - not just what they buy
- Speak your boundaries with love - and stick to them

Business Tips for the Legacy-Driven Leader

- Use email, speaking, or storytelling platforms to amplify your voice
- Build community-based offers - memberships, retreats, group programs
- Set clear client communication policies to protect your energy
- Don't downplay your soft skills - package them as your unique advantage
- Collaborate with people who love structure so you can shine in connection

Remember: your gift isn't just creating connection - it's building trust that turns communities into movements.

Ready to Go Deeper?

You've uncovered your **Relationships & Communication Energy**. Next, we'll explore the archetypes that naturally align with this energy - so you can lead, speak, and connect in ways that feel authentic, sustainable, and powerful.

Because your ability to build trust, spark conversation, and create belonging?
That's your brilliance. And the world needs more of it.

Discover Your Archetype Quiz

Instructions: For each question, choose the answer that feels most true for you. Trust your gut - the first instinct is usually the right one!

1. When working with others, you feel most energized by:

A) Sharing ideas clearly and making sure everyone's on the same page.

B) Meeting new people, building relationships, and finding connections.

C) Creating harmony and making sure everyone feels comfortable and included.

2. People often describe you as:

A) Articulate, persuasive, and great at explaining things.

B) Friendly, outgoing, and well-connected.

C) Calm, diplomatic, and a natural mediator.

3. When conflict arises, you tend to:

A) Step in to clarify misunderstandings and keep communication flowing.

B) Bring in different people or resources to help resolve it.

C) Quietly diffuse tension and help everyone find common ground.

4. Your favorite part of networking events is:

A) Speaking or presenting to the group.

B) Mingling, exchanging cards, and discovering new opportunities.

C) Observing and stepping in to help conversations go smoothly.

5. In a team project, you naturally:

A) Lead discussions and ensure ideas are communicated clearly.

B) Connect people who might not otherwise meet or collaborate.

C) Check in on everyone's feelings and keep the peace.

6. The biggest frustration for you in business is:

A) Miscommunication or people not listening.

B) Feeling disconnected or out of the loop.

C) Tension or conflict that disrupts the team's flow.

7. You feel most fulfilled when:

A) Your message resonates and inspires action.

B) You've built meaningful relationships or made valuable connections.

C) You've helped people understand each other and find common ground.

8. Under stress, you're more likely to:

A) Try to talk things through until there's clarity.

B) Reach out to your network for support or ideas.

C) Withdraw a bit to avoid escalating tensions.

9. Your superpower is:

A) Finding just the right words to express what others are thinking.

B) Building bridges between people and opportunities.

C) Calming situations and helping people feel understood and valued.

10. True success, to you, means:

A) Using your voice to influence and inspire others.

B) Knowing a wide circle of people who support and uplift each other.

C) Creating environments where everyone feels safe and connected.

Scoring

- Mostly A's → You're The Communicator.
- Mostly B's → You're The Networker.
- Mostly C's → You're The Peacemaker.

Archetypes in This Energy of Brilliance™

The Communicator

Welcome to the realm of resonance, empathy, and eloquence. The Communicator is the bridge-builder - the voice that transforms tension into trust and silence into shared understanding. You don't just hear people - you truly listen. You help others feel seen, known, and safe enough to speak their truth.

Think of **Oprah**, whose gift for presence created a global platform where vulnerability became strength. Or **Lin-Manuel Miranda**, whose artful storytelling invites people to feel and *connect* in unforgettable ways. Like them, you hold the power to spark transformation - not by force, but by fostering meaning and mutuality.

Your ability to translate complexity into clarity, and emotion into insight, makes you the glue that holds people and purpose together. But while your voice brings people in, it's vital to remember: your *own* voice deserves just as much space, too.

How to Spot a Communicator

- Always knows who's feeling what - even when no one's saying it.
- Naturally steps in to translate between two people talking past each other.

- Uses words like "let's clarify," "how does that feel?" or "tell me more."
- Keeps conversations inclusive so everyone has a voice.
- Sometimes leaves a meeting thinking, *did we actually decide anything?*
- Secretly worries about being "too nice" or "too much."

Strengths

- Articulate and clear in expressing ideas.
- Excellent listener and empathetic mediator.
- Builds trust and fosters team cohesion.
- Skilled at navigating sensitive or emotional conversations.
- Creates spaces where people feel valued and heard.

Shadow Side

- Avoids conflict or tough conversations to maintain peace.
- Can over-accommodate, sacrificing their own priorities.
- Risks endless dialogue without reaching decisions.
- May soften messages too much to avoid offense.

Emotional Cost (Internal)

Your words uplift, inspire, and connect - but constant giving can leave you speechless in all the wrong ways. When your energy dips, you might feel:

- Emotionally wrung out from holding space without getting it back.
- Invisible despite always amplifying others' voices.
- Stuck in mental loops, overthinking how you came across.

- Guilty for needing silence or solitude when you're known for being "the supportive one."
- Unseen when you finally speak your truth - and it's not received with care.

Remember: When this happens, you might quietly pull back - avoiding messages, hesitating to reply, or even feeling paralyzed by the pressure to "say it right." Your voice is powerful - but your presence doesn't require constant performance. Silence can be sacred, too.

Stress Triggers (External)

- High-conflict or emotionally charged group dynamics
- Being pressured to "fix" interpersonal tension
- Getting interrupted, dismissed, or talked over
- Rapid decisions made without collaboration
- Being asked to explain, defend, or mediate when you're already drained

Growth Tips (When to Ask for Help)

When your gift for connection starts to feel like a burden, ask yourself:

- What truth needs to be spoken - even if it's uncomfortable?
- Am I leaving space for my own voice and boundaries?
- Who can help me turn these conversations into concrete action?
- Am I carrying emotions or burdens that aren't mine to hold?
- Where can I simplify instead of overexplaining?

Remember: true harmony isn't about avoiding conflict - it's about moving through it with respect and honesty.

Least Compatible (But Also Most Growth-Expanding)

Say hello to your favorite frenemy: The Executor.

You're gently making sure everyone's voice is heard, while the Executor is tapping their watch saying, "Let's just get it DONE."

Executors may view Communicators as overly verbose or indecisive. Communicators may feel Executors bulldoze through important emotional or interpersonal nuances.

But when paired with mutual respect? You create harmony *and* forward motion.

Try this mantra:

"Clarity drives action, and action needs clarity."

Dream Team Suggestions

Your voice is vital - but you don't have to carry every conversation alone. Here's your ideal crew:

- **The Strategist**: Brings long-term vision to shape your conversations with purpose
- **The Executor**: Turns discussions into decisive action
- **The Catalyst**: Infuses energy and forward momentum when conversations stall

- **The Analyst**: Grounds your insights with data and logical perspectives
- **The Organizer**: Keeps conversations structured and ensures follow-through

Bottom line: You bring the human touch - your team helps transform it into collective progress.

Business Wisdom for the Communicator

Your voice isn't just heard - it moves people. You don't just talk, you connect, uplift, and translate vision into impact.

Here's your brilliance-in-action alignment guide:

- Speak up - even when your voice shakes. Your truth creates space for others to do the same.
- Embrace clarity as a form of compassion - directness saves time, confusion, and heartache.
- Protect your energy - emotional labor is real, and boundaries are brilliance-preserving.
- Partner with executors - your words deserve to be backed by action.
- Use your message with intention - when you speak with purpose, people lean in.

✅ Own your role as the Communicator. You're not just here to speak - you're here to bridge, guide, and activate.

☑ Don't second-guess your tone - your intuition knows how to connect.

☑ Trust that your gift isn't noise - it's nourishment.

Your brilliance turns conversation into change and empathy into action. You don't just speak - you spark transformation.

A note to you: Communicator, your words are more than filler - they're fuel. You give language to what others feel but can't express. But remember you don't need to carry every conversation. Protect your peace. You're not too emotional, too soft, or too much. You're the frequency that lifts ideas into alignment. Let your voice be heard, honored, and echoed. The world *needs* your clarity.

The Networker

Welcome to the world of buzzing conversations, unexpected introductions, and the magic of human connection. The Networker is sociable, charismatic, and fueled by genuine curiosity about people and possibilities. You're the kind of person who turns a random coffee chat into a collaboration - and somehow always knows someone who knows someone.

Think of **Reid Hoffman**, who co-founded LinkedIn to help people make meaningful career connections. Or **Arianna Huffington**, co-founder of The Huffington Post, whose influence and people-centered mindset turned into movements, media, and communities that have changed conversations around well-being and leadership. Like them, you intuitively see that relationships are the ultimate resource - and you know how to build them like nobody else.

But your brilliance can also come at a cost: pulled in too many directions, running on half-finished conversations, or feeling burnt out by always being "on." The magic happens when you learn to channel your people power with intention - and let your network work *for* you.

How to Spot a Networker

- Talks to strangers in elevators - and actually enjoys it
- Can't help playing "human matchmaker," personally or professionally

- Thrives on events, conferences, and any excuse to meet new people
- Says, "I know someone who does that!" about almost everything
- Has a phone full of contacts - and remembers personal details about all of them
- Finds isolation torturous and hates feeling "out of the loop"

Strengths

- Brilliant at building and nurturing authentic relationships
- Connects people and ideas for mutual success
- Naturally persuasive and engaging in conversation
- Spots new opportunities through diverse networks
- Creates vibrant communities where people feel seen and included

Shadow Side

- Can spread themselves too thin across too many relationships
- Risks neglecting follow-through on commitments
- May prioritize networking over focused, deep work
- Sometimes skims the surface instead of going deep on fewer priorities

Emotional Cost (Internal)

Your magic lies in weaving people together - but when overextended, you might feel:

- Scattered by too many surface-level interactions
- Guilty for falling behind on follow-ups or forgetting key connections

- Disconnected from your purpose, even as you stay "plugged in"
- Lonely, because few relationships feel mutual or nourishing

Remember: When this builds, you might feel tempted to vanish from every group chat, thread, or event invite. That's not failure - it's a signal. Your brilliance isn't measured by how many people you reach - it's in the depth of the connections you choose to nurture.

Stress Triggers (External)

- Isolation from teams or long solo work stretches
- Work cultures that discourage conversation or collaboration
- Projects with no room for feedback, partnership, or exchange
- Feeling sidelined in decisions or team dynamics
- Pressure to "be on" socially when your cup is already empty

Growth Tips (When to Ask for Help)

When your calendar's packed and your mind is racing, pause and ask:

- Which relationships truly deserve my time and energy right now?
- Who can help me turn connections into tangible outcomes?
- Am I keeping my promises - or just making more introductions?
- Where might fewer, deeper conversations serve me (and others) better?
- How can I create healthy boundaries, so my networking doesn't drain me?

Remember: The goal isn't to know everyone - it's to build relationships that *matter*.

Least Compatible (But Also Most Growth-Expanding)

Say hello to your favorite frenemy: The Specialist.

You're all about expanding connections and broadening horizons. The Specialist thrives in a deeply focused niche, often preferring depth over breadth.

Networkers may see Specialists as withdrawn or uninterested in social engagement.
Specialists might view Networkers as scattered or too surface-level.

But when you meet in the middle? You combine social spark with technical substance.

Try this mantra:

"Depth is as valuable as breadth - and we can help each other shine."

Dream Team Suggestions

You bring the people - now let the right crew help you activate the impact:

- **The Communicator**: Helps clarify your message and deepen rapport
- **The Catalyst**: Brings energy and momentum to turn connections into action
- **The Strategist**: Helps you prioritize relationships that align with long-term goals

- **The Organizer**: Keeps your network organized and ensures follow-up happens
- **The Visionary**: Inspires you with big ideas worth rallying people around

Together, this team transforms your people skills into practical results.

Bottom line: You're the spark that gets things moving - this team helps make sure your connections turn into real momentum.

Business Wisdom for the Networker

You're not just building contacts - you're weaving a web of possibility. Your presence turns introductions into opportunities and conversations into collaborations.

Here's your brilliance-in-action alignment guide:

- Choose quality over quantity - your magic shines brightest in aligned connections.
- Schedule intentional time for deep work - your brilliance doesn't require being "on" 24/7.
- Follow through - when action meets access, your network becomes a superpower.
- Create space for reciprocity - relationships flourish when the energy flows both ways.
- Protect your peace - your vibe is valuable, but it's not a vending machine.

☑ Own your role as the Networker. You're not just well-connected - you're a connector of dreams, ideas, and purpose.

☑ Don't chase every opportunity - curate the ones that feel like a full-body yes.

☑ Trust that your presence is the invitation, and your discernment is the filter.

Your gift is turning connection into momentum. You don't just meet people - you move them.

A note to you: Networker, your energy is magnetic. You gather, you uplift, and you create the kind of synergy most people only dream about. But you don't have to be available to be valuable. You don't need to collect - just connect, with care. When you slow down, your impact deepens. Let your network be a garden, not a hustle. Legacy grows from intentional relationships - and yours are meant to bloom.

The Peacemaker

Welcome to the heart of calm in the storm. The Peacemaker is gentle, diplomatic, and deeply committed to helping people feel seen, heard, and safe. You're the one who notices when someone goes quiet in a meeting, who steps in to ease tension, and who reminds everyone - sometimes without saying a word - that kindness is a strength, not a weakness.

Think of **Desmond Tutu**, whose work in post-apartheid South Africa modeled forgiveness without forgetting, and **Fred Rogers**, whose quiet voice carried generations through emotional literacy and self-worth. Like them, you radiate trust. You listen when no one else will. And you help people find their way back to each other when things get hard.

But your steady presence can come at a cost. In your beautiful desire to keep the peace, you might stay silent when something hard needs to be said. You may carry the burden of others' emotional needs without anyone realizing it. Know this: your peacekeeping is a gift - but your truth matters just as much.

How to Spot a Peacemaker

- Checks in with people after tense meetings
- Starts sentences with, "I understand where you're coming from…"
- Believes harmony is worth working for - even when it's hard
- Notices emotional undercurrents nobody else sees

- Often gets asked, "Can you help mediate this?"
- Secretly wishes everyone would just get along

Strengths

- Natural mediator who resolves tension with grace
- Creates safe, inclusive spaces for diverse voices
- Deeply empathetic and perceptive
- Maintains morale and unity, even under stress
- Encourages collaboration and mutual respect

Shadow Side

- May avoid necessary confrontations to keep things smooth
- Can become indecisive trying to please everyone
- Risks burying personal needs or opinions
- Sometimes struggles to set or enforce clear boundaries

Emotional Cost (Internal)

Your calm exterior often conceals a well of quiet tension. When you overextend, you might feel:

- Emotionally numb from internalizing too much unease
- Unappreciated because you're always steady, never dramatic
- Disconnected from your own needs after over-accommodating others
- On edge, like you're constantly anticipating the next emotional blow-up
- Angry - but unsure how to express it without rocking the boat

Remember: You might smile, nod, or say "it's fine" while craving silence and space. Peacekeeping doesn't mean self-abandonment. You deserve restoration, not just resolution.

Stress Triggers (External)

- Loud environments with dominant personalities
- Being caught in prolonged or unresolved conflict
- Pressure to take sides when neutrality feels safer
- Being expected to make everyone comfortable at your own expense
- Sudden emotional demands that require instant response or soothing

Growth Tips (When to Ask for Help)

When you're feeling torn between keeping the peace and speaking your truth, ask yourself:

- What am I not saying that needs to be heard?
- Who can help me navigate this conversation with courage?
- Am I avoiding short-term discomfort at the cost of long-term harmony?
- How can I assert myself while staying true to my compassion?
- Is silence protecting others - or keeping me small?

Remember: your empathy and diplomacy are gifts. And sometimes, the bravest path to peace starts with speaking up.

Least Compatible (But Also Most Growth-Expanding)

Say hello to your favorite frenemy: The Specialist.

You're tuned into team dynamics and emotional well-being. The Specialist is focused, detail-driven, and prefers deep solo work in their niche.

Peacemakers may feel shut out or dismissed by the Specialist's disinterest in group harmony.

Specialists may view Peacemakers as overly emotional or distracting from "the real work."

But when you learn to honor each other's language - feelings vs. facts - you create solutions that are both smart and sustainable.

Try this mantra:

"Technical brilliance and human connection both matter. We just shine in different ways."

Dream Team Suggestions

Your calming energy is priceless, but you don't have to hold it all alone. Your ideal team includes:

- **The Catalyst**: Brings momentum and courage when tough conversations are needed
- **The Strategist**: Helps you see the long game and weigh outcomes clearly
- **The Executor**: Turns peaceful resolutions into real-world action
- **The Innovator**: Offers creative solutions for resolving tension
- **The Mentor**: Provides steady wisdom and reminds you to take care of yourself, too

Together, this team helps you maintain harmony *while* driving progress.

Bottom line: You restore balance - your team ensures that balance leads to bold, lasting change.

Business Wisdom for the Peacemaker

Your presence calms storms, smooths edges, and reminds people that business can be human. You create safety - and that's what makes transformation possible.

Here's your brilliance-in-action alignment guide:

- Speak up, even when it feels uncomfortable - your truth brings clarity, not conflict.
- Set boundaries with love - protecting your energy helps you show up with strength.
- Embrace healthy tension - it's often the pathway to authentic connection.
- Advocate for yourself as fiercely as you advocate for others.
- Don't mistake harmony for hiding - your voice belongs in every room you're in.

☑ Own your role as the Peacemaker. You're not here to avoid discomfort - you're here to model what grace looks like in hard conversations.

☑ Don't minimize your leadership style - it's powerful because it's grounded in empathy.

☑ Trust that your inner calm is a catalyst for outer change.

Your gift is turning conflict into connection, and silence into healing.

A note to you: Peacemaker, your gentleness is a strength - not a liability. You hold space like few can. But don't forget, peace isn't the absence of noise - it's the presence of truth. Your voice matters. Your needs matter. And when you honor both, you don't just keep the peace... You lead with it.

Guidance & Support Energy

"Where holding space becomes strength - and your presence becomes power."

If you've landed here, you probably hear this a lot:

"You just get me."

"I don't know how, but you always make me feel better."

"You're the only one I can talk to about this."

Sound familiar? Then welcome home. This is the Energy of Brilliance™ where empathy meets leadership - and compassion becomes a catalyst for transformation. You aren't just a good listener. You're a wisdom-keeper. A truth-speaker. The one who steadies the room when emotions run high and reminds others of their brilliance when they forget.

I know this Energy intimately. I've carried it across industries, late-night client calls, and quiet personal moments of doubt. It's powerful - and sometimes heavy. But here's the truth: you're not here to carry everyone. You're here to guide. You're not here to fix people. You're here to walk with them until they remember they were whole all along.

Why This Energy of Brilliance™ Matters

In a world that glorifies hustle, hype, and constant noise, your energy is the exhale. The pause. The recalibration.

You remind people that it's okay not to have it all figured out - and that they're not alone while they figure it out.

And that is life-changing.

Your brilliance creates:

- **Safe spaces** where vulnerability isn't a weakness - it's the doorway to growth
- **Deep relationships** built on trust, truth, and shared humanity
- **Sustainable success** because people feel supported, not pressured
- **Business cultures** that prioritize emotional intelligence alongside results

But yes, it can be draining. You might:

- Feel invisible because you're working behind the scenes
- Worry you're being "too soft" for business
- Take on emotional weight that wasn't yours to carry
- Wonder who holds space for *you*

So let me say this loud and clear:

- Your softness is strength.
- Your steadiness is strategy.
- Your presence is power.

How This Energy Might Show Up for You

If this is your Energy, you may:

- Be the first to notice when something's "off" in a person or process
- Feel most fulfilled when you're helping others rise
- Struggle to separate your worth from your ability to support others
- Thrive in one-on-one relationships and deep, heartfelt conversations
- Feel depleted when people mistake your care for weakness

You're the mentor, the coach, the nurturer, the emotional backbone. Whether it's teaching, healing, advising, or encouraging - your work creates ripples that last.

Your Brilliance in Action

At your best, you:

- Help others believe in themselves again
- Foster deep loyalty from clients, partners, and team members
- Bring calm to crisis, and hope to hard moments
- Lead with integrity, heart, and intentionality
- Make people feel seen, safe, and supported

You don't just guide.

You *elevate*.

What Fuels You

You feel energized when you have:

- One-on-one time to truly connect
- Opportunities to encourage and uplift

- Space to reflect and recharge
- Environments that value empathy and authenticity
- Clients or collaborators who appreciate emotional intelligence

What Might Drain You

This Energy can burn out when faced with:

- Constant emotional labor with no boundaries
- Being expected to "fix" everything for everyone
- Feeling undervalued because your work isn't always quantifiable
- Too much noise, pressure, or conflict without reprieve
- A lack of appreciation for the *way* you lead

You don't need to be louder.

You need to be honored for who you are.

Your Strengths

- Deep empathy and intuitive insight
- Building meaningful, lasting relationships
- Providing emotional safety in professional spaces
- Helping others access their potential
- Supporting steady, values-aligned growth

Your Growth Opportunities

- Feeling responsible for everyone's well-being
- Struggling to set boundaries without guilt
- Underestimating the value of your "invisible" labor
- Putting others' needs before your own for too long

- Doubting your leadership because it's rooted in care

Remember: your heart is not a weakness - it's a compass.

Tips for Thriving in This Energy

- Build in rest and boundaries as non-negotiables
- Work with others who can handle logistics while you handle people
- Document the emotional labor you're doing - it has business value
- Share your insights and reflections as part of your content or offer
- Receive support as much as you give it - mentors need mentors, too

Business Tips for the Heart-Led Leader

- Create offers that reflect your strengths - like 1:1 sessions, retreats, or coaching containers
- Use your story and empathy as marketing superpowers - people trust people
- Package your wisdom - turn insights into guides, courses, or frameworks
- Systematize emotional support (like check-in emails, client journeys, etc.)
- Choose aligned clients who value your approach and respect your energy

Ready to Go Deeper?

You've uncovered your **Guidance & Support Energy**.

This Energy doesn't need to shout to be heard - it leads by being present, grounded, and deeply human.

And in this Energy, one archetype rises above the rest: **The Mentor**.

So instead of a quiz, flip to the next section to explore how The Mentor archetype becomes the heartbeat of business - and the soul of real, lasting impact.

You don't just hold space.

You shape futures.

The Mentor

Welcome to the circle of steady guidance, deep wisdom, and the sacred act of helping others grow. The Mentor is nurturing, intuitive, and anchored in a calling to pour into others - gently guiding them toward their full potential. You bring not just information, but transformation: through your stories, your presence, and the patient way you hold space for others to rise.

Think of **LeVar Burton**, who inspired millions of children to fall in love with reading and believe in their own brilliance. Or **Maya Angelou**, whose mentorship transcended generations through poetry, activism, and soul-deep truth. You, dear Mentor, are the soul of legacy - the one who sees the greatness in others long before they believe it for themselves.

But your steady approach can sometimes clash with the rapid pace of today's world. While you aim to shield others from unnecessary mistakes, you may resist new ideas or feel frustrated when your experience is overlooked. Still, know this: your wisdom *is* relevant - especially when paired with openness to evolution.

How to Spot a Mentor

- Often asked, "Can I get your advice on something?"
- Believes that growth takes time - and is worth the wait
- Shares lessons through stories, metaphors, and experience

- Offers reassurance while holding people to their highest standard
- Struggles with fast, chaotic change
- Deeply moved when someone says, "You changed my life"

Strengths

- Offers wisdom and perspective rooted in experience
- Invested in developing and empowering others
- Patient, supportive, and deeply encouraging
- Builds long-term trust and loyalty
- Balances emotional support with practical advice

Shadow Side

- May resist untested methods or unconventional ideas
- Can be overly directive, believing there's "one right way"
- Sometimes imposes personal values or outdated systems
- May struggle to adapt quickly in rapidly evolving environments

Emotional Cost (Internal)

You lead with wisdom and care - but the weight of being the steady one can take a toll. When your energy dips, you might feel:

- Invisible in rooms that prize trends over truth
- Undervalued when advice is ignored or unacknowledged
- Weary from being the emotional anchor for everyone else
- Disheartened watching others stumble after not taking your insight to heart

Remember: You're not failing when others don't listen - you're still planting seeds. But even the strongest guides need their own safe harbor.

Stress Triggers (External)

- Fast-paced environments that move without reflection
- Being overlooked in favor of flashy or new ideas
- Teams that seek advice but never implement it
- Constant change without time to mentor or adjust
- Dismissiveness toward experience, tradition, or long-game thinking

Growth Tips (When to Ask for Help)

When your roots feel steady, but your branches need a stretch, ask yourself:

- What can I learn from someone newer or different than me?
- Am I offering guidance - or controlling the outcome?
- Is there space for others to discover their *own* answers?
- How can I keep evolving while staying grounded in my truth?
- Who mentors *me* - and how can I lean into that support?

Remember: great mentors never stop learning. Your legacy is not about knowing everything - it's about growing with grace.

Least Compatible (But Also Most Growth-Expanding)

Say hello to your favorite frenemy: The Catalyst.

You value patience, process, and reflection. The Catalyst charges ahead, fueled by inspiration, intuition, and a need for motion.

Mentors might view Catalysts as impulsive, unfocused, or dismissive of consequences.

Catalysts might see Mentors as too slow, overly cautious, or rigid in their approach.

But together, you can make magic: bold innovation grounded in wisdom.

Try this mantra:

"Speed and stability can coexist. We grow stronger when we grow together."

Dream Team Suggestions

Your wisdom becomes unstoppable when paired with the right team. Surround yourself with:

- **The Visionary**: Sparks new horizons and keeps your guidance future-focused
- **The Implementer**: Translates your wisdom into consistent, practical action
- **The Networker**: Expands your influence and connects you with those who need your guidance
- **The Analyst**: Grounds your advice in data and structured insight
- **The Communicator**: Ensures your stories and teachings land with clarity and heart

Bottom line: You nurture growth. Your team amplifies it. Together, you shape impact that lasts for generations.

Business Wisdom for the Mentor

Your quiet confidence, lived experience, and emotional intelligence make you a guiding light for others. You don't need to be the loudest in the room to have the most impact - your presence *is* the strategy.

Here's your brilliance-in-action alignment guide:

- Trust the pace of transformation - real growth takes time, and you're here for the long haul.
- Release the urge to rescue - guidance lands best when it's invitational, not instructional.
- Embrace feedback as a mirror - it helps refine your message, not reduce your wisdom.
- Let your evolution be visible - your vulnerability becomes someone else's permission slip.
- Don't shrink your impact - legacy is built through presence, not perfection.

☑ Own your role as the Mentor. You are a stabilizing force in chaos, a gentle reminder that growth is possible even when life feels messy.

☑ Don't underestimate the value of your lived experience - what you've overcome becomes your curriculum.

☑ Trust that your words, when rooted in love and truth, create a ripple effect that you may never fully see.

Your gift is the ability to *see people not just as they are - but as they're becoming.* You plant seeds of belief, offer steady roots, and remind others of their potential, even when they forget it themselves.

A note to you: Mentor, you were never meant to blend in. Your calm isn't passive - it's powerful. And while others may chase the spotlight, you build something more lasting: trust. You lead through love, consistency, and alignment. When you trust your voice - and allow yourself to evolve with the times - you don't just offer wisdom.

You *embody* it.

Blending Your Energies of Brilliance™

Discovering Your Unique Mix

Your brilliance is like a diamond - multi-faceted, ever-evolving, and uniquely yours. While your **Primary Energy of Brilliance™** forms the foundation of how you lead, create, and show up in the world, it's not the whole story. Most people don't fit neatly into one box - and that's a *good* thing.

In fact, if you scored high in more than one energy, you likely embody a **Primary Energy** and a **Secondary Energy**, each with its own set of archetypes that shape how your brilliance flexes depending on context. That adaptability is what helps you thrive in seasons of change, collaborate with others, and avoid burnout while still delivering your best.

What Does Your Blend Look Like?

Think of your **Primary Energy of Brilliance™** as your default setting - the way you approach life and business when you're aligned and resourced. Within that Energy, you'll have one **Primary Archetype** (the one you scored highest in) and possibly a **Secondary Archetype** (your runner-up within the same Energy). That blend already gives you nuance.

But if your results show a second Energy scoring close behind your Primary, congratulations - you've got a **Secondary Energy of Brilliance™**, too. This is the part of you that shows up when:

- A new environment demands different strengths
- You're leading through a crisis or transformation
- You're collaborating and flexing with others' energy
- Your Primary Energy is feeling undernourished or overused

You'll then explore **your Secondary Energy** the same way: identify your top archetype (and if applicable, your secondary archetype within that Energy). This approach reflects how layered, dynamic, and real you are.

Example:

Let's say your Primary Energy is **Strategy & Foresight**, and your strongest archetype is **The Analyst** with a secondary of **The Specialist**. You're deeply logical, data-driven, and love mastery.

But your results also showed a strong connection to **Relationships & Communication**, especially **The Communicator**. That becomes your Secondary Energy and archetype.

Now you know you lead with insight - but deliver it in an emotionally resonant, human-centered way. You're not just strategic; you're relatable. That's your edge.

How to Spot Your Blend in Action

Your Secondary Energy or archetype may quietly power you in the background - or take center stage when needed. You'll know it's active when:

- You solve problems differently than usual
- You notice a shift in your energy or habits
- You're feeling both excited and stretched

- Your usual instincts feel off, and a new rhythm emerges

Instead of boxing yourself in, blending your Energies of Brilliance™ allows you to evolve. It's your secret weapon for:

- Leading with flexibility and empathy
- Making better decisions (because you're self-aware)
- Building offers, routines, and systems that actually work for *you*
- Showing up authentically in business, even as you grow

Tips to Honor Your Energetic Range

- **Name both energies.** Say them out loud. Write them in your journal. Own them.
- **Check in with both.** Before major decisions, ask: What would my Primary do? What is my Secondary asking me to consider?
- **Use Them Wisely.** Lead with your Primary but bring in your Secondary when you need a shift in approach or energy.
- **Use your blend intentionally.** Bring your secondary forward in spaces where your primary might get drained.
- **Rest Differently.** Each energy refuels in its own way. Know how to recharge both parts of your brilliance.

Cross-Reference Table

Here is a simple cross-reference for each primary Energy of Brilliance™ and the way it might shift depending on your secondary.

Primary Energy	Secondary Energy	What That Blend Might Look Like
Creativity & Future	Structure & Implementation	*Visionary with a plan* - You dream boldly, but also know how to break it into steps.
Creativity & Future	Strategy & Foresight	*Innovative with insight* - You imagine what's next and back it with strategy.
Creativity & Future	Relationships & Communication	*Empathetic creator* - You connect through your ideas and inspire others to act.
Creativity & Future	Leadership & Support	*Bold changemaker* - You spark new paths and naturally rally people behind your vision.
Structure & Implementation	Creativity & Future	*Grounded dreamer* - You keep things running but still make room for innovation.

Primary Energy	Secondary Energy	What That Blend Might Look Like
Structure & Implementation	Strategy & Foresight	*Master planner* - You organize both people and possibilities with ease.
Structure & Implementation	Relationships & Communication	*Relational anchor* - You create structure that supports connection and trust.
Structure & Implementation	Leadership & Support	*Anchor of action* - You manage the details and keep everyone aligned and steady.
Strategy & Foresight	Creativity & Future	*Future-ready innovator* - You plan with purpose and aren't afraid to reimagine.
Strategy & Foresight	Structure & Implementation	*Methodical visionary* - You see the path and take measured steps toward it.
Strategy & Foresight	Relationships & Communication	*Insightful storyteller* - You blend data and emotion to move hearts and minds.

Primary Energy	Secondary Energy	What That Blend Might Look Like
Strategy & Foresight	Relationships & Communication	*Insightful storyteller* - You blend data and emotion to move hearts and minds.
Strategy & Foresight	Leadership & Support	*Purpose-driven guide* - You lead with clarity, precision, and quiet confidence.
Relationships & Communication	Creativity & Future	*Inspiring connector* - You light people up and make them feel seen and heard.
Relationships & Communication	Structure & Implementation	*Steady communicator* - You create reliable pathways for others to thrive.
Relationships & Communication	Strategy & Foresight	*Strategic listener* - You guide conversations with intention and meaning.
Relationships & Communication	Leadership & Support	*Supportive influencer* - You lead gently, helping others rise without force.

Primary Energy	Secondary Energy	What That Blend Might Look Like
Leadership & Support	Creativity & Future	*Vision-led nurturer* - You coach with creativity and care.
Leadership & Support	Structure & Implementation	*Operational wisdom* - You lead behind the scenes, calmly moving things forward.
Leadership & Support	Strategy & Foresight	*Wisdom-forward mentor* - You help people see their blind spots with love.
Leadership & Support	Relationships & Communication	*Culture builder* - You lead from the heart and create environments where others feel safe to thrive.

In the next section, you'll explore how to:

- Lean into your strengths with intention
- Collaborate more effectively with others
- Build teams that complement your brilliance

Let's keep building. You're not meant to do this alone - you're meant to do it aligned.

Working with Your Brilliance

How to Lean into Your Strengths

Let's start with a truth I hope you hold close:

There is absolutely nothing wrong with how you're wired.

The way your brain fires with possibilities… the way you instinctively care, build, question, plan, or inspire… none of that needs to be fixed. It needs to be *honored*.

And yet - if you're anything like me or the brilliant humans I've coached - you've probably had moments where you questioned that wiring. Maybe you've whispered things like:

- *"I'm too much…"* because your ideas never sleep.
- *"I'm not enough…"* because you'd rather listen than lead with volume.
- *"I should be more strategic, more consistent, more confident…"* insert whatever "not enough-ness" has followed you.

But hear me loud and clear:

You don't need to become someone else. You need to trust who you already are.

Working with your archetype is about designing your business, your offers, and your leadership style to fit like a glove - not a cage.

Here's what that might look like in real life:

- A **Visionary** posting one idea-driven message per week instead of forcing a rigid content plan.

- An **Implementer** setting systems in motion without feeling pressure to "wing it" like others do.
- A **Communicator** turning stories into sales - not with pressure, but with presence.
- An **Analyst** finding peace (and power) in a well-built spreadsheet that shows what's *really* working.

When you move in alignment with your Energy of Brilliance™, you stop resisting your flow - and start amplifying it.

How to Collaborate with Other Archetypes

One of the most freeing truths in business?

You're not supposed to do it all.

You're not broken because you need support - you're wise. Collaboration isn't a weakness; it's a superpower.

Every archetype brings something essential to the table. Instead of comparison, we get to cultivate *complementarity*. For example:

- **Visionaries** need **Organizers** to anchor their ideas into timelines.
- **Executors** come alive when paired with **Innovators** who reframe the problem.
- **Peacemakers** soften the friction that **Catalysts** sometimes spark.
- **Specialists** bring depth while **Networkers** bring fresh doors to open.

When you learn to speak each other's language, you build partnerships rooted in mutual brilliance - not power struggles.

Try this:

- If you're a **Peacemaker**, call on a **Catalyst** to help push forward an idea you've been sitting on.
- If you're a **Visionary**, lean on an **Implementer** to help reverse-engineer your big dream.
- If you're an **Analyst**, partner with a **Communicator** to translate your insight into impact.

You don't have to *be* every archetype.

You just need to understand how to dance with the rest.

Why All Archetypes Are Valuable in Business

Let me say it louder for the perfectionists in the back:
There is no "best" archetype.

Without Visionaries, we'd never innovate.

Without Executors, we'd never launch.

Without Communicators, no one would feel connected.

Without Peacemakers, teams would crumble.

Without Analysts, we'd keep repeating mistakes.

And so on.

Every archetype fills a gap that another can't. This isn't about being well-rounded alone - it's about being well-supported. Together, we build businesses that are resilient, creative, clear, and *human*.

How Knowing This Makes You a Better...

Leader

You lead with integrity because you know where you shine - and where you need others to shine with you. You stop trying to copy what's not yours and inspire others by showing up as yourself.

Collaborator

You speak with empathy, knowing not everyone processes the same way.

You don't just work together - you co-create. That's where the magic happens.

Marketer

You communicate in your own voice. Whether you are story-driven, data-informed, or systems-led, you stop chasing trends and start resonating with the people meant for you.

Decision-Maker

You recognize how you make decisions - and how your team or clients do, too. You stop second-guessing and start choosing with clarity and trust.

What Comes Next

You've met your archetype. You've explored your Energy of Brilliance™. Maybe even a few surprise blends sparked your curiosity.

Now, it's time to move from insight to integration.

Because knowing who you are is only part of the journey - the next step is building a life and business that *moves* with that knowledge.

Not harder. Not faster. Just… smarter. More soulfully. More *you*.

This next chapter is about aligning your strengths with the right support - *the kind that doesn't just lighten the load but expands your capacity.*

It's about cultivating a circle that fuels you rather than drains you.
A team, a community, a rhythm where everyone's brilliance can breathe.

You don't have to be every archetype.
You don't have to carry it all.

You simply have to *honor how you're wired* - and surround yourself with people who do the same.

So, let's dive into what that can look like.

Because building a business with ease, joy, and flow?
That's not a dream - it's your next move.

Can You Be All the Energies of Brilliance™?

Why You're *Not* Meant to Be Everything

(Even If You're Scarily Good at Everything)

Let's get real for a second.

Just because you *can* do it all… doesn't mean you should.

I say this with love - and from lived experience.
Because I was that woman. The one juggling every role, every archetype, every Energy of Brilliance™ like a performance art piece no one even asked for.

In higher education? I was the behind-the-scenes fixer, turning professors' chicken-scratch diagrams into digitized brilliance.

In hospitality? I dreamed up a profit-generating pre-order gifting platform for hotel guests - long before "upselling" became a thing. And when it got dismissed? That's when I learned something the hard way: **being visionary isn't enough when the room isn't ready for it.**

And for a long time, I wore every hat. Strategist. Implementer. Networker. Visionary. Etc.....
It made me adaptable… but it also made me tired.
And sometimes? It made me feel like a stranger to myself.

So let me offer this truth to you gently but clearly:

- You don't need to master all the Energies of Brilliance™.

- You don't have to morph into every archetype to be worthy.
- And no, being "multi-passionate" does *not* mean you're meant to carry it all alone.

The Caution You Need to Hear

Here's the danger:

When you try to be everything to everyone, you start losing the parts of you that matter most.

You burn out. You shrink. You over-function.
And what's worse? You begin to believe the lie that your brilliance only matters if it *looks like* someone else's.

But friend, hear me now:

- You don't have to be the whole engine.
- You just need to know your gear - and run in it with power.

You were never meant to do business (or life) solo. Your energy was designed to *plug in*, to *complement*, to *collaborate*. That's the brilliance of the framework - it's not a personality box; it's a blueprint for building together.

So instead of asking, *"How can I do it all?"*, ask:

- What am I uniquely gifted to lead?
- Where does my energy thrive without force?
- Who can I partner with so we both shine brighter?

Because yes - you *can* grow. You *can* expand. You *can* evolve.

But not from a place of pressure. From a place of **choice**.

And there's nothing more powerful than a woman who knows what's hers to carry - and what's not.

So, before you keep flipping pages or jumping to "fix" a gap…

Pause.
Breathe.
Celebrate the brilliance you *already* bring.

This is your permission slip to stop proving - and start aligning.
You don't need to wear all five Energies like badges of honor.
You just need to know yours - and trust that your people are out there, bringing the rest.

Let's build a business that doesn't require you to shapeshift to succeed.
Let's build one that feels like home.

Be brilliant,
Vanessa

Ready to stop doing it all and start building the support you deserve?

Flip to the next chapter: *Building Your Dream Team* - where you'll learn how to align your strengths, fill in the gaps, and co-create success with people who complement your brilliance beautifully.

Building Your Dream Team

How to Assemble a Balanced Team

Let me tell you something I've learned - sometimes the hard way:

No one builds a business that lasts by doing it all themselves.

In the early days, I believed I had to be the planner, the strategist, the marketer, the implementer, and the customer whisperer - all at once. And honestly? I *was* all those things. I figured it out. I built systems. I kept the wheels turning.

But even with all that resourcefulness, I hit a wall. Because being the glue *and* the engine *and* the fuel? That's a recipe for burnout.

Building your dream team isn't about growing fast or hiring a dozen people at once. It's about alignment.

It's about finding people whose brilliance complements your own.

It's about building trust, not just talent.

And it's about letting people shine in the roles they were *meant* to own.

A balanced, energy-aligned team includes:

- **Big-picture thinkers** who ignite new ideas and possibilities
- **Practical doers** who bring those visions to life step by step
- **Detail-oriented anchors** who catch the small things that matter
- **Relationship builders** who keep the culture thriving and the people connected

When all these energies work together - not in competition, but in harmony - your business doesn't just grow.

It becomes magnetic. Sustainable. And deeply human.

Using Your Archetypes to Hire, Partner, or Collaborate

Here's the beauty of understanding your own Energy of Brilliance™: It's not just a self-awareness tool - it's a roadmap for building better relationships in business.

When you know where you shine *and* where you might dim, you gain clarity. Suddenly, hiring that Virtual Assistant, choosing the right collaborator, or figuring out what kind of support you need next... gets easier. And smarter.

You stop guessing. You start aligning.

Here's a guide to pairing your dominant archetype with complementary ones - because magic happens when you bring together strengths that *balance*, not just match:

Visionary

Partner with Executors, Implementers, or Strategists.
These teammates help you bring your bold, beautiful ideas out of your head and into the world - with timelines, steps, and accountability that keep you grounded.

Innovator

Look for Executors, Implementers, or Communicators.

They'll help shape your trailblazing ideas into tangible offerings, while keeping you from spiraling into endless what-ifs.

Analyst

Seek Visionaries, Communicators, or Implementers.

They'll add spark and movement to your methodical brilliance - turning insights into action and clarity into momentum.

Strategist

Collaborate with Executors, Innovators, or Communicators.

These partners keep your long-term vision alive while bringing the creative juice and people-savvy energy needed to move your plans forward.

Specialist

Team up with Visionaries, Communicators, or Organizers.

They'll help elevate your deep expertise, expand your reach, and translate your brilliance into offers that serve others.

Communicator

Work with Strategists, Executors, or Catalysts.

These allies give your words direction, transform messages into movements, and ensure your storytelling gets results - not just reactions.

Networker

Pair with Communicators, Catalysts, or Strategists.

Together, you'll turn connections into collaborations, and community into conversions - while staying focused on the bigger picture.

Peacemaker

Seek out Catalysts, Strategists, or Mentors.

These partners bring decisive energy and strategic guidance, helping you make moves when you'd otherwise wait for harmony to magically arrive.

Catalyst

Collaborate with Communicators, Innovators, or Executors.

They'll help you pace your fire, focus your energy, and transform your momentum into lasting progress - not just quick sparks.

Organizer

Join forces with Visionaries, Communicators, or Implementers.

They'll inject creativity and fluidity into your systems without throwing off your sense of order - bringing freshness without chaos.

Executor

Work with Innovators, Communicators, or Strategists.

These teammates keep your action-oriented energy aligned with purpose and possibility, making sure you're not just busy - you're building.

Implementer

Pair with Visionaries, Analysts, or Communicators.

They'll stretch you beyond "what's always worked" and help tie your precision to purpose-driven growth that feels expansive *and* doable.

Knowing these archetypes helps you go deeper than surface-level resumes or networking scripts.

You stop asking *"Can they do the job?"* and start asking:

- "How will they approach it?"
- "Do their strengths fill the gaps I'm carrying too long?"
- "Will their energy balance mine - or quietly clash?"

And here's the truth that many miss:

Your "least compatible" pairings might be the very ones that transform your business.

When navigated with grace, curiosity, and clear communication, those dynamics become your secret weapon.

So, as you dream up your next hire, collaboration, or partnership, remember this:

- You're not building a carbon copy of yourself.
- You're building a collective of brilliance.

And the most extraordinary teams aren't made up of people who think the same - **they're made of people who grow together.**

Interview Questions to Identify Archetypes

Whether you're interviewing a potential hire, exploring a new collaboration, or just getting to know someone over a latte at your favorite café - understanding archetypes can give you powerful clues about how someone will show up in business.

These questions aren't about ticking boxes. They're about *listening beneath the answers* - for energy, for patterns, for brilliance waiting to be matched with the right role or relationship.

You're not just looking for *what* they do…
You're uncovering *how* they think, create, solve, and connect.

Here are conversation starters to help you do just that:

Visionary

"What's an idea you're passionate about - even if others think it's a little out there?"
"When a challenge comes up, do you focus on fixing it now - or envisioning what's possible in the long term?"
"Do you enjoy exploring trends, even if they aren't immediately useful?"

Organizer

"Tell me about a time you created a system or routine that made life or business smoother."

"Do you feel most confident when everything's planned - or when there's room to adjust on the fly?"

"How do you usually respond when plans go off track?"

Executor

"When you join a project, do you naturally start taking action - or wait for direction?"

"What's your relationship with to-do lists or checkboxes - love them or loathe them?"

"How do you stay steady when priorities start shifting around you?"

Implementer

"Do you prefer established processes - or do you like tweaking things as you go?"

"Tell me about a time you took an idea and made it happen - step by step."

"Do you enjoy repetitive tasks if they lead to consistency and stability?"

Innovator

"What's something you've improved or redesigned just because you saw a better way?"

"Do new ideas come to you easily - even if they seem unconventional?"

"How do you balance dreaming big with actually finishing things?"

Analyst

"When making a decision, do you start with intuition or information?"

"What kinds of data or details do you naturally pay attention to that others might overlook?"

"Can you share a time when your analysis helped prevent a costly mistake?"

Strategist

"Do you gravitate toward daily execution - or mapping out future goals?"

"How do you help a team connect today's work to tomorrow's outcomes?"

"Have you ever paused a project because it didn't align with a long-term plan?"

Specialist

"Is there something you've mastered over years of focus and study?"

"Do you prefer being the go-to expert in one area - or wearing lots of hats?"

"How do you stay connected to a team when you're deep in your own zone?"

Communicator

"Are you someone who speaks up easily - even about tricky topics?"

"Do people often ask you to help explain things in a way that makes sense?"

"What's your approach to resolving tension during a tough conversation?"

Networker

"Do you get energized meeting new people - or prefer a small, close circle?"

"Can you tell me about a time your connection led to a big opportunity?"

"What helps you keep relationships strong across a big network?"

Peacemaker

"How do you usually respond when there's conflict on a team?"

"Do you often find yourself smoothing things over or helping others compromise?"

"When tensions rise, do you take action - or wait to see how things unfold naturally?"

Mentor

"Do people often seek your guidance or lean on you for advice?"

"What lights you up about helping others grow?"

"Are you more hands-on as a guide - or do you like to empower others to find their own way?"

These questions aren't meant to label anyone - they're designed to *reveal their rhythm.*
Pay attention to the stories they tell, the language they use, and what makes their energy light up. You'll start to see their Energy of Brilliance™ come through loud and clear.

Because when you choose people based on alignment - not just resumes - you build a team that works in harmony, plays to each other's strengths, and *actually enjoys the process.*

And that, my friend, is the foundation of a business that thrives.

How Different Archetypes Complement Each Other

One of the most beautiful (and sometimes frustrating!) parts of building a dream team is this:

We're all wired differently.

Your way of thinking, creating, or communicating might feel second nature to you - but to someone else? It's *totally foreign.* And vice versa.

That's why understanding archetypes is so powerful. It gives you language for what's working, where the friction is, and most importantly - *why.*

When you recognize the way each Energy of Brilliance™ moves through the world, you stop expecting everyone to operate like you. You start seeing people as puzzle pieces - each bringing a shape that completes the bigger picture.

But let's be real: sometimes the pieces don't snap into place right away. Compatibility doesn't always mean *easy.*
Sometimes the best teams grow through a little bit of tension, curiosity, and mutual stretch.

Here are some powerful pairings - and the growth Opportunities they bring:

Visionaries & Organizers

Visionaries dream boldly. Organizers bring the structure to execute. One without the other? Chaos or stagnation.

Together? Magic.

Growth Opportunity: Visionaries can feel boxed in by systems. Organizers can get overwhelmed by constant change. But when they collaborate with trust, vision turns into sustainable momentum.

Catalysts & Analysts

Catalysts are all go, go, go. Analysts want to pause and double-check the data.

Together? Smart speed.

Growth Opportunity: Catalysts need to slow down. Analysts need to move forward before every risk is eliminated. Their tension? Totally normal - and totally valuable.

Communicators & Executors

Communicators stir energy and inspire. Executors ground the plan and *make it happen.*

Together? Words in motion.

Growth Opportunity: Communicators may want to "talk it out" a bit too long, while Executors are ready to dive in. But with clarity and shared timelines, they make a phenomenal team.

Mentors & Networkers

Mentors love deep growth. Networkers love broad reach.

Together? Expansive transformation.

Growth Opportunity: They both give a lot - sometimes too much. The magic happens when they balance nurturing others with protecting their own energy.

Specialists & Peacemakers

Specialists dive deep. Peacemakers hold space.

Together? Seamless integration.

Growth Opportunity: Specialists may want solitude; Peacemakers thrive in connection. But when they bridge the gap, expertise meets harmony in powerful ways.

Innovators & Implementers

Innovators spark change. Implementers ground it in reality.

Together? Progress with purpose.

Growth Opportunity: Innovators may chase the next shiny idea. Implementers may resist pivoting. But when they respect each other's rhythm, they create *lasting* innovation.

Strategists & Catalysts

Strategists look ahead. Catalysts act now.

Together? Fire with direction.

Growth Opportunity: They might clash over timing. But with mutual respect, they balance visionary planning with bold execution.

Analysts & Visionaries

Analysts love logic. Visionaries chase possibilities.

Together? Big dreams, backed by data.

Growth Opportunity: Visionaries may overlook details. Analysts may overanalyze risks. Together, they turn intuition into impact.

Organizers & Communicators

Organizers set the structure. Communicators keep everyone aligned.

Together? Clarity in motion.

Growth Opportunity: Organizers crave precision. Communicators love nuance. But together, they create smooth systems *and* team harmony.

Executors & Peacemakers

Executors move fast. Peacemakers keep the team balanced.

Together? Results with heart.

Growth Opportunity: Executors may push too hard. Peacemakers may avoid tension. But when they sync, they get things done *without burning bridges*.

Here's the truth: **Your team doesn't need every archetype.**
But it does need *complementary* styles - people who balance your blind spots, stretch your strengths, and keep you accountable to what matters.

And those tricky pairings? The ones that *rub a little*?
They're not problems. They're opportunities for brilliance.

Because when we learn to *respect* each other's energy instead of trying to "fix" it - we unlock a whole new level of trust, creativity, and power.

Before You Move On...

Building your dream team is about more than hiring or outsourcing - it's about choosing alignment over exhaustion, collaboration over control.

When you intentionally surround yourself with people who complement your Energy of Brilliance™, everything shifts:

- You stop carrying the weight alone.
- You start operating in your zone of genius.
- You unlock momentum you didn't even know was missing.

And the beautiful part? The team you need might not look how you expected. Sometimes the people who challenge your style are the exact ones who stretch your brilliance and expand your capacity.

So, let what you've learned here settle in.

Revisit your own archetype.

Reflect on the roles and energies still missing from your circle.

And get curious: *Who belongs at your table next?*

Because the next chapter isn't just about what you've discovered - it's about what you'll *do* with it.

Let's talk about where you go from here.

Bringing Your Brilliance to Life

So here we are - at the close of this book, but truly just the beginning of your next chapter.

You've taken a courageous first step: you've begun to **_Decode Your Brilliance™_**.

You've uncovered your Energies of Brilliance™, explored how you're wired to lead and create, and started aligning your business with your natural strengths.

But insight alone isn't enough - the magic happens when you turn that insight into action. And the beautiful part? You don't have to do it alone.

Want to keep decoding your brilliance and building a business that reflects the real you?

Workshops

These aren't your average training sessions. They're part strategy session, part soul-reboot - filled with real talk, powerful prompts, and implement-now tools. Whether you're launching, pivoting, or scaling, you'll leave with clarity and confidence.

Cocoon Circle Membership

A gentle, guided space for women ready to stay connected to their purpose and momentum. Inside, you'll get:

- **The Source Drop** – your monthly brilliance booster, packed with prompts, insights, and visibility tips
- **Positive Energy Calls** – light-touch live sessions to recharge and reflect
- **Spotlights & Directory Access** – visibility support and opportunities to connect with fellow changemakers

This is your monthly cocoon for inspired growth and aligned strategy.

Mariposa Makers Membership

For those ready to go deeper and do business their way - without the burnout. Includes everything from Cocoon Circle *plus*:

- A private **Energy Check-In Call** each month to decode your progress
- **Early access to collab opportunities**, publishing projects, and VIP experiences
- **Weekly co-working sessions** so you don't just plan - you *do*

This is where your momentum meets a community that truly sees you.

1:1 Coaching

If you're ready for personalized, eyes-on-you support, this is for you. We'll build strategy around **your brilliance**, your energy style, and your vision - not someone else's template. Whether you need clarity, structure, or the courage to step into something new, I'm here to walk with you.

No pressure, no perfection required - just a place to keep growing, your way.

Start here: linktr.ee/mariposasources

One Final Reflection

You've started decoding your brilliance - and that alone is something to celebrate.

But more than that, you've reminded yourself of something vital:

- You are not too much.
- You are not behind.
- And you are allowed to build a business that works the way you do.

So don't stop here. Keep decoding, keep experimenting, and most of all - keep honoring the way your brilliance wants to move through the world.

Your next step isn't about doing more. It's about aligning more deeply with what already lives inside you.

Because you're not here to fit a mold.

You're here to *rewrite the rules* - and to lead with brilliance that's fully, unmistakably yours.

Let's keep going.

With heart, strategy, and soul,

Vanessa

About the Author

Vanessa Siliezar is a business strategist, storyteller, and the founder of **Mariposa Sources**, a community-driven space where purpose meets practicality. With over 20 years of experience across industries - from higher ed to hospitality, government to grassroots entrepreneurship - Vanessa brings a rare gift: the ability to decode complex ideas and translate them into empowering, doable strategies that help people work *smarter*, not harder.

She's not your average business coach. Vanessa is a transformation guide - known for helping women and creative entrepreneurs uncover their strengths, simplify their systems, and step fully into their brilliance. Whether she's guiding a nonprofit leader, a boutique owner, or a multi-passionate dreamer, she meets them with clarity, compassion, and bold belief.

Her journey has taken her from executive assistant to international consultant, from grieving daughter to generational legacy-builder. Armed with a Master's in Business Management and a calling bigger than any job title, Vanessa founded Mariposa Sources to make entrepreneurship more human, more sustainable, and more joyful - especially for women rewriting the rules.

She lives in Southern California with her son Brandon and her partner David, where you'll often find her listening to music from empowering artists like Peachkka or Toni Jones, creating Canva magic, or dreaming up ways to infuse heart into hustle. She carries her father's wisdom with her daily and believes that when we rise, we rise together.

Decode Your Brilliance™ is her invitation to you:

- To stop fitting into boxes you've outgrown.
- To lead from your strengths, not your shoulds.
- To build a business - and a life - that fits *you*.

Let's keep the momentum going: linktr.ee/mariposasources